THE LAST VOICES

WORLD WAR II VETERANS OF THE AIR WAR SPEAK MORE THAN HALF A CENTURY LATER

ELIZABETH CASSEN

The Last Voices

World War II Veterans Of The Air War Speak More Than Half A Century Later

Self-published by Elizabeth Cassen

Printed by CreateSpace

ISBN: 0996154000
ISBN-13: 978-0996154000

DEDICATION

To these men, and all of our veterans who deserve our highest praise and deepest thank you for a job well done.

To my parents, Allan Weston Crowell and Elizabetha Matzenbacher Crowell, who were loyal, hardworking and caring members of this generation.

To my husband, Mark Cassen, a great aviator in his own right, having flown everything from a Cessna 150 to the Boeing 747-8F aircraft.

CONTENTS

ACKNOWLEDGMENTS

The author is grateful for the support from the following individuals:

Pattie McLaine, Catharine Gill, Katharine Ball, Richard C. Robert, George and Barbara Snook, Arthur Kemp, Ed and Lois Carter-Edwards, Charles I. Williams, Ernest and Sherry Rosser, Everett and Merrilyn Culp, Howard "Tommy" Thompson, Jack and Bonnie Kingsley, Molly Kingsley, Nancy S. Barnes, Len Chaloux, Marion and Bernita Hoffman, Michael Pivarnik, Denise Pivarnik-Nova, Jim Pivarnik, Paul Ross, Gailard "Red" Ketcham, Clarence and Dodie Stearns, Norman and Pauline Hall, John Hall, Norm Burmaster, Randy Kemp, Mark Cassen, Dr. Mary Neal and Alex Alexe.

INTRODUCTION

Mindful of the fact that over six hundred World War II veterans are passing away each day, according to recent figures from the Veterans Administration, I set out on a series of road trips across the United States and Canada to photograph, and hear the stories of some of the survivors.

This project began on an impromptu basis. As a retired pilot from a major U.S. airline, I attended some of the final reunions of flying squadrons from the war, beginning with the seventieth anniversary of the Doolittle Raid, held at Wright-Patterson Air Force Base in Dayton, Ohio. I talked with some of the airmen, including B17, B24 and B25 crewmembers who served over the European theater, and realized I must do my part to preserve their experiences. Conversations with one veteran would lead to referrals to others.

My parents were of the Great Depression/World War II generation, each born just prior to 1920, in two different countries that later again would be at war with each other. My father, a conservative New England gentleman, was exemplary of his generation, family oriented, patriotic, hard-working, obedient toward authority, devoted to volunteer and church work, optimistic with common "horse sense," though not deeply philosophical.

My German-born mother carried many emotional burdens common to immigrants in a strange new country. She arrived in America at the tender age of 4, by ship, in the arms of her parents, who were emigrating in 1923 to escape the harsh realities of the German Weimar hyper-inflation. Her father, a master tailor, hoped to find work and a new life in New York City. Due to the German hyper-inflation, it was impossible for a tailor, (or any service-provider), to make a profit. Once the material was ordered, and the suit or garment was made, the price for the material far exceeded the original price quoted to the customer. This was unsustainable for the head of a young family, and a major change had to be made. Although life was not easy in New York City upon arrival, my grandparents and mother became loyal, contributing U.S. citizens for the rest of their lives.

My folks each studied hard, went to work after their schooling, and met and married in Massachusetts at war's end in 1945. My mother shipped her wedding dress and other clothing back to Germany, well aware that the German people literally had nothing, after bombing caused widespread destruction in all the major cities. The war killed millions of soldiers and civilians and destroyed the economy.

One comes to realize that the action of ordinary people pushing themselves to the maximum of their abilities more often dictate the great moments, than the actions of famous leaders or wealthy people. General Dwight D. Eisenhower was quoted in the book "The First Heroes", by Craig Nelson, as stating "Higgins was the man who won the war for us". Andrew Higgins was a boat builder from New Orleans who invented and mass-produced thousands of plywood, flat-bottomed ramp barges used during D-Day at Normandy, France, and all over the world.

The men and women of the Great Depression who came of age in World War II made lasting sacrifices in the war. When I walked the beaches of Normandy in the mid- 1990s and viewed the thousands of neat rows of white headstones spanning over miles, I realized how much I am indebted. The most humbling and emotional experience is to walk along their final resting place. It is written that 292,131 Americans were killed in action in the war, most young and far from home. They now rest in cemeteries all over the world, many in fields in unmarked graves. Often, their families and loved ones never learned what became of them.

During the war, there was never a time in American history when so many citizens were working and living toward a shared cause. The same is true of Canada, as you will see from my interviews with Canadian veterans. Canada was, of course, part of the British Commonwealth.

The annual reunions of military units from the war are getting smaller now, some veterans prefer not to make the trip, or cannot, due to health reasons. I hope more of the stories will be preserved as reminders of their sacrifice and all that we owe them.

Each chapter relates the unique experience of an American or Canadian veteran, either serving as a pilot or crewmember on a bomber serving over Europe or the Pacific, or someone tied into the aviation aspect of the war. I wished to concentrate only two theaters of the war, maintaining a consistent subject matter. As the project progressed, by chance I was given the name of another airman I "should talk to", and it took a life of its own. Interviewing these gentlemen was very enjoyable, with a feeling of familiarity, as I was talking with men who grew up in the same decades as my own parents. Some very unexpected stories came to light, tying into infamous events of the war, with surprises along the way. Included in the book are stories associated with the infamous events: bombing on D-Day; flying under the direction of the famed actor, Jimmy Stewart; one man's story of being imprisoned in the notorious Buchenwald concentration camp with 167 other airmen; the story of Senator Robert Dole's war injuries as told by one of the interviewees; an airman who dove head-first out of a burning B-17 only to be captured by the Germans; memories of flying with the Tuskegee Airmen, from the man then the oldest living member; and many other historical stories. I thank each gentleman I met in the course of this project for their service to their country. It is an honor to know them. They returned home, building the society we have today.

All the gentleman interviewed for this project are true heroes, all with medals and honors that reflect their service. Some gentlemen were more forthcoming about their awards, some preferred not to mention them; therefore, for consistency, I have generally not listed each award or rank each serviceman received. They are all deserving of our appreciation and great respect. The quotation at the heading of each chapter is one that has special meaning for that particular gentleman.

The afterword illustrates a living example of how we may remain involved today in carrying the history forward. Read the efforts of a dedicated group of veterans and volunteers, restoring a B-17 in a hangar at Grimes Field, Urbana, Ohio, a decade long project. Their efforts form a tight camaraderie among the team, leading to participation in many programs and events each year.

And now, some amazing stories of courage, heroism and persistence...

CHAPTER 1

"Abandon all hope, ye who enter here"
- Dante, Inferno
(Sign over the door to the pilot briefing room at
"Old Buckenham", England)

Dick Robert is a very lucky man, having survived without a scratch 35 bombing missions as a B-24 tail- gunner over Europe during World War II. Unwavering persistence led to his acceptance into the Army Forces (Air Corps) Aviation Cadet Training Program, and active combat over Europe.

Richard C. Robert was born in 1921, growing up on the family sugar cane farm near White Castle, Iberville Parish, Louisiana. Although this was a considerable distance from any airport, Robert caught the "aviation bug" at an early age and enthusiastically collected aviation magazines. At the time of the attack on Pearl Harbor, he was living in a Baton Rouge boarding house, working for the Louisiana Department of Highways as an engineering aide on a highway survey party, as well as a volunteer member of the Baton Rouge Civil Air Patrol as a certified airman.

Shortly after turning 21 in January 1942, Robert volunteered at the Baton Rouge Army Air Base at Harding Field, hoping to enter the Aviation Cadet Program. Cadets were required to be in excellent overall physical condition for acceptance, and he was told some work needed to be done on his teeth. This was completed, and upon return to the base, was then informed his pulse was too high, resulting in rejection for medical reasons. Undaunted, Robert then volunteered for the Cadets in New Orleans, a two-hour ride from Baton Rouge by train, which he took at his own

Robert-Aviation Cadet Glendale AZ April 1, 1943

expense. Someone had told him to take aspirin before his next medical exam to slow down his pulse, and upon finishing another three days of intensive medical, physiological and flying aptitude testing, he passed on February 25, 1942. The Cadet call-up process took much longer than Robert anticipated, and having resigned from his job in Baton Rouge, he accepted a position as an Engineering Survey Party Chief in the Louisiana Department of Public Works branch office in nearby Plaquemines. In late April, after not hearing back from the Cadet board, Robert wrote a letter to the Army Air Forces. He received a letter in late May instructing him to return to the New Orleans recruiting office for further processing, and at the end of the month, was sworn in as an Army Air Force Enlisted Reservist. He returned home, and continued working with the surveying party.

In late October, Robert received another letter instructing him and 18 other reservists to report to New Orleans for appointment as aviation cadets on November 2, 1942. The next day, they were on a train headed to California for preflight training, which Robert said was a "very unique, interesting and

2

luxurious train trip;" he had never before been further west than Houston. Because of secrecy involved with war operations and troop movements, the new cadets were not allowed to tell anyone they were leaving. An open air platform on the rear of the train enabled him to watch the mountain and desert scenery.

B 24 Crew. Robert bottom row far right.

Upon arrival in California, the new recruits were driven 40 miles south of Los Angeles to Santa Ana Air Base for initial training, which consisted of further testing and medical exams to determine whether each man would enter into training to become a pilot, navigator or bombardier. Robert said the 12-week school was similar to a college level math and science cram course. The cadets also studied basic navigation, Morse Code, aviation and military fundamentals, and identification of Allied and enemy airplanes and warships. The daily routine included strenuous physical activity, consisting of close order drills, marching and calisthenics. The recruits were also taught how to bail out of airplanes by jumping from a high ground tower using open parachutes attached to the tower by cables. Robert said military physical training was far easier than his previous drainage surveying work back in the Louisiana swamps.

At the same time, an old friend, Charles Hamilton, was in bombardier training at the school, and the two young men frequently visited Hollywood, including the famous theaters and nightclubs. They enjoyed the Hollywood Palladium Ballroom, a night club with a capacity of over 6,000 people that featured well known bands. A scarlet fever quarantine in 1943 prevented the cadets from using their tickets to the Rose Bowl game between UCLA and the University of Georgia. Robert noted that the Hollywood movie stars and residents were all very gracious to the Armed Forces personnel.

Next came Primary Flight School in Phoenix, Arizona, for nearly three months. Robert was informed by the Army Air Force that he would make an excellent commercial airline pilot, but was not suited to military flying, and was then sent to radio operator school in South Dakota and aerial gunnery school in Texas for eight months. In December 1943 he graduated as an aerial gunner and shortly thereafter was assigned to a B-24 heavy bomber aircrew as a tail turret gunner. The crew completed their B-24 phase training on March 26, 1944, at Muroc Army Airbase, California. While there, the men had to sign their last will and testament and were not allowed to leave the room until they had done so. Robert recalled, "Being only 23, that really shook me up!" They were then transferred to Hamilton Field, just north of San Francisco, to receive their overseas assignment.

Leaving from Morrison Field in West Palm Beach, Florida, on April 8, 1944, Robert and his new bomber crew set out on their long overseas flight to Wales in a new B-24 Liberator. Passing over Puerto Rico, they were required to refuel at San

Lucia Island, before spending the night in Trinidad. They flew to Belem, Brazil, the next day, and spent the night. The following day they crossed over the Amazon River, the Equator, Devil's Island, (an infamous prison on the French Guiana coast), and landed in Natal, Brazil. There, vendors sold often-defective goods to the airmen, because they correctly assessed that by the time the purchase proved faulty the airmen would have already moved on. Robert purchased a watch that failed 10 hours later. A 12-hour flight took them to Dakar, French West Africa, where the crew stayed five days. Extremely tall black men guarded the aircraft while it was parked. The next leg of the trip took them across the Atlas Mountains to arrive at Marrakech, French Morocco. The final leg crossed the Atlantic around the European coast, passing Portugal, Spain, and France for arrival at Valley, Wales, where the plane was taken and sent for modification. Bad weather led to a trip of 13 days, with 56 flying hours.

A train carried the crew to Stone, England, where they stayed at a Combat Crew Replacement Center for six days, then on to Scotland, and then on by boat to Ireland. After four days of aerial gunnery school the crew attended six more days of the same in Greencastle, Ireland. On May 16, Robert's crew traveled to Old Buckenham, England, a B-24 bomber base, about 100 miles north of London. At the base, the crew was assigned to the 734th Squadron, 453rd Group, 2nd Air Division, 8th Air Force.

At that time, the Eighth Air Force was the largest worldwide, consisting of three Air Divisions separated into 40 heavy bomber groups. The Second Air Division consisted of 14 bomb groups, each group usually divided into four bomb squadrons, each containing a minimum of 12 bombers. There would be about 48 bombers on an airfield, in striking distance of the Luftwaffe. Therefore, when the bombers were not in use, they were parked around the edges of the airfield, so as to minimize damage in the event of an attack. Each bomb group was under the command of a full colonel, supervising about 3,000 airmen and ground personnel. The flight crews lived in Quonset huts, constructed of semi-circular cross-sections of corrugated steel, spartanly equipped with 12 beds and a heater, with two crews to a hut. They were provided with English-style cots and three pillows; for extra comfort, Robert sewed the pillows together into a makeshift mattress. Officers lived nearby in a wooden building, in private rooms.

The Eighth Air Force, performing daytime bombings, alternated with the Royal Air Force, which did night bombings. Still, the wakeup call for the day bombings was given in the middle of the night for mission preparation. The men had to shave, dress, eat breakfast, attend the mission briefing, don their flight suit and equipment, ride to the far side of the airfield, then check equipment. The B-24 was an unpressurized aircraft, and a close shave was important for a tight seal in wearing the oxygen masks. Eating a large breakfast was also crucial, as missions could last eight or more hours, and only small snacks such as a sandwich and candy bar were carried on board.

The briefing room featured a wall map of Europe, which was unveiled after the start of the briefing, revealing the route of flight marked by a long red ribbon. The briefing would cover information on the target, expected enemy opposition, en-route time, and time over the target. The routes were planned to best avoid enemy ground anti-aircraft guns.

The airmen would then move to the equipment room to put on their flight gear, including temperature adjustable heated flight suits, three types of gloves (leather, wool, and silk), heavy fleece-lined flight boots, oxygen mask, parachute harness, flight helmet equipped with a throat microphone, headphones and goggles, a 20-pound flak (anti-aircraft artillery) vest, and steel helmet. The throat microphones controlled the oxygen mixture and flying suit heat. Sometimes Robert's heart rate increased dramatically under the stress of the mission, and he learned to lower the heat in the flight suit and raise the oxygen level to compensate. The pilots had a small floor heater up front, but the aircraft was basically open to the outside air temperatures, sometimes as low as -60 F. Also provided were life preservers, a parachute and an escape kit for each man, which consisted of European money, compass, multi-lingual phrase book, (French, Dutch, German and Spanish languages included), and small civilian photographs of themselves for obtaining fake identification papers. Robert also placed a tube of toothpaste in his kit, but after it exploded at altitude, he replaced it with tooth powder for the rest of the airborne missions!

Upon arrival at the aircraft, each crewmember had a standard preflight check appropriate for their station. The gunners checked the gun turret operating systems, ammunition supply, and machine guns. Essential to the mission were completely dry machine guns and turret systems, as any moist equipment, including machine gun mechanisms, could freeze at altitude, in spite of electronic heating pads. All bomber crew members carried .45 caliber semi-automatic pistols in either a shoulder holster or a cowboy-style belt holster on combat missions. Robert carried his .45 under his arm in a shoulder holster, and slept with his weapon under his pillow (which was his fleece-lined flight jacket) at night. The men were told German paratroopers might infiltrate their base during the night, and to be prepared to defend themselves.

Two 50-caliber machine guns equipped with a computing gun sight were mounted in the tail turret, and the turret rotated virtually 180 degrees, providing the gunner with complete mobility for defense against threats from the aircraft rear. The tail gunner was protected by 2 ½-inch thick reinforced glass in the upper section, and a 2-inch thick armor plate below. A steel helmet and flak suit were still necessary items due to the thin steel and plexi-glass construction of the rest of the turret. A portion of the flak suit was an apron laid across the gunner's lap, but because most flak originated from below, the apron did not protect from any fire, so Robert sat on the flak apron. Also, each B-24 bomber carried one .45 caliber Thompson sub-machine gun, and one thermite canister in the waist, for use in an emergency landing to set the plane on fire to prevent the Germans from capturing a bomber. However, Robert and the two waist gunners were concerned that the thermite canister would explode if hit by flak, and thereby cause an in-flight fire, so they routinely dropped it overboard when crossing the English Channel. No one in authority at the base ever mentioned the missing thermite canisters.

After preflight completion, the aircraft scheduled to fly the mission would line up by squadron, take off one by one, and climb to a set altitude. The aircraft would then circle around a radio beacon, assembling first by squadron, then by group, combat wings, and finally, as the Eighth Air Force. A 1,000-aircraft force would require an airborne assembly time of about two hours. Then the force would fly over the English Channel, and all crew members would don their oxygen masks upon reaching 10,000 feet. The machine guns would be test fired to ensure proper working order. Robert recalled that "the bomber stream, which might extend to 15 to 20 miles long, had to be at 20,000 feet when they reached the continent to lessen flak accuracy."

On May 24, 1944, Robert flew his first mission in a plane called "Notre Dame" to Orly Airfield, Paris, France. Robert did not know what to expect on his first mission. The men observed some "pretty colored smoke," and until the first bit of flak hit the aircraft, the new crew did not realize the smoke was caused by anti-aircraft fire. Robert later said, "Although we were trained, you can't practice people shooting at you." The Liberators on the mission that day attacked airfields at Orly and

Melun, south of Paris, and Ceil, northeast of Paris, unchallenged by German fighters, although they were met with moderate flak.

A week later, Robert's crew was flying an older, battle-weary B-24 on a mission to Oldenberg, Germany, when an engine caught fire over the English Channel. Aborting the mission, the pilot sounded the bell, ordering the crew to bail out. The waist gunners bailed out immediately, being in the position from which to most easily go. In the meantime, the pilot was able to extinguish the fire, and turned off the alarm. No other crew members bailed, and the pilot landed at an emergency base. The two waist gunners showed up back to base the next day. Upon landing with parachutes, they had been surrounded by English farmers wielding pitchforks, and it took a bit a time to convince the farmers they were Americans, as one of the gunners was of German descent.

The crews were all eager to participate in the invasion of the European continent, which would come on D-Day -- June 6, 1944. The men felt they would face little opposition in the air, and wanted to assist the ground troops. Early in the morning, the crew was awakened by the squadron orderly, and told to be where they ate the typical breakfast of fried eggs, bacon and other greasy food. Immediately after, they reported to the combat crew briefing room for a detailed briefing on the target of the day. James M. "Jimmy" Stewart (more about the famed actor in the next chapter), at that time a lieutenant colonel, was the Air Operations officer assigned to Robert's bomb group, and flew routinely as a command pilot on different aircraft, but was not assigned to a particular crew. Lt. Col. Stewart gave a very dramatic briefing for the invasion. In the briefing room, roll was taken, the doors locked and a large cloth covering the mission map was removed. Everyone on base had been anxiously waiting for the Allied invasion of France, not knowing when it would occur, and on that day, the men knew they would have the honor of participating in the history-making invasion of enemy-occupied France. There was considerable excitement among crews in the briefing room. The Eighth Air Force carried out three separate missions on D-Day. The first wave, in which Robert participated, involved more than 1,300 B-24 Liberators and B-17 Flying Fortresses in a 6 a.m. attack that lasted an hour and a half. Robert recalled, "The entire English Channel was covered with ships." More than 100 targets were bombed at the German coastal defenses. Robert's squadron was then sent to Caen, France, to assault German communications. The second mission involved a group of heavy bombers assaulting a defended position behind the coastline at Coutances. The third mission was carried out by Liberators to defend another interior location. Many bombers returned back to base with their payloads intact, because poor weather and visibility caused reluctance to drop bombs where Allied troops were possibly positioned. Robert's crew completed their mission, encountered no flak, and returned to base.

Inexperienced bomber crews were usually given older, worn aircraft to fly until a good number of missions were completed. After six completed missions, Robert's crew was assigned a new B-24 bomber, which they named "Hollywood and Vine." They named it after the famous intersection, as a reminder of many enjoyable weekends spent in Hollywood during their B-24 training in California, and the co-pilot, a commercial artist, drew the logo on the plane.

For each completed bombing mission, a small bomb was painted as part of a row on the left side of the plane's nose. Each crew member's leather jacket had the name of the plane and a caricature painted on the back. Small painted bombs would be added after each successful mission, showing how much combat a crew member had seen. Most four-engine bomber pilots were only in their late teens or early twenties, and there was close camaraderie. Some missions were back-to-back, and sometimes there were several days between missions.

Early model B-24s did not have fixed Plexiglass waist windows. Therefore, in order to use the waist machine guns, the metal windows had to be propped open on bombing missions, creating very cold conditions in the rear of the airplane. By D-Day, Robert's crew was given a newer model airplane with fixed Plexiglass windows in the waist, allowing the machine gun barrels to project through a small opening in the Plexiglass.

On June 12, 1944, Robert's next mission was to be the largest Allied attack since D-Day, with more than 7,000 sorties flown. More than 1,400 heavy bombers attacked 16 German airfields and six French bridges. The bombers encountered little flak and met no enemy fighters in an attack ranging from the Paris outskirts to Saint Lo. Robert's crew bombed an airfield bridge in Montfort. Three radio and flak towers, 17 enemy aircraft, 11 trains, 63 railway cars, 102 trucks, and a tank were destroyed by the fighter escort accompanying the bombers.

Robert's bomb group was sent on June 20 to a Politz, Germany, a synthetic oil plant. More than 1,500 Liberators and Flying Fortresses attacked other oil plants in Hamburg, Ostermoor and Magdeburg, as well as a Sallersleben wing repair factory, and a tank depot in Konigsburg. Robert's 453rd group faced intense enemy flak, and 60 to 70 five enemy fighters, although his plane itself did not. Another bomber group lost nearly all of their aircraft. Despite heavy opposition, the Politz raid resulted in an overall success. Sixty tons of bombs were dropped by all Allied aircraft; Robert said this was the roughest mission he flew.

When Robert shut the access door to his tail gunner position at the rear of the aircraft, the isolation from the rest of the crew necessitated in the use of an intercom. During the Politz mission return trip, his crew had been unable to make contact with him. He could hear them talking, but they could not hear him. One of the waist gunners, believing that Robert might be dead, came back to take a look. The two discovered that flak had cut the intercom system wires connecting to the tail turret.

The most dangerous time of each mission was when the aircraft was directly over the target flying straight and level to drop the bombs, and attacks were most likely to occur then. Robert's plane was only directly attacked on a few occasions, but he witnessed heavy damage to others. Body armor provided much protection for the men, but there was no way to prevent flak from striking the plane. Flak could also hit their dropping bombs, causing them to detonate immediately, destroy the plane, and often take out other planes as well. As Robert accurately observed, "There are no foxholes in the sky."

On June 21, Robert's crew joined more than 1,000 heavy bombers for the first large-scale attack on Berlin since D-Day. The 453rd bomb group was assigned to attack a FW (Focke-Wulf) 190 engine factory. Other targets included factories and railway yards. So many aircraft flew over Berlin at one time that pilots had to follow prearranged air traffic patterns. Approximately 50 ME (Messerschmitt) 410s , ME109s, JU (Junkers) 88s, and FW 190s attacked a single B-24 group, and another wave of 50 JU 88s struck a B-17 attack force wing. Robert's crew was able to successfully defend themselves against ME190s and ME410s. Despite the German attempt to cover Berlin with a smoke screen, the bomber crews were still able to see their targets and complete the mission with great accuracy.

Robert was included in a force of 571 B-24s on July 18, in cooperation with the 9th Air Force and Royal Air Force, to bomb troop concentrations and German equipment over an area of more than 70 square miles in Caen, France. In slightly over three hours, between 7,000 and 8,000 tons of bombs were dropped. The British Second Army was leading the attack over

Caen, and the rest of the forces were included for broad support. Robert's group of Liberators arrived at the target site about 7:45 a.m., releasing more than 1,400 tons of bombs in 30 minutes, most of them fragmentation Type, which do not make large craters. The mission was completed with the great accuracy required, as at one point the Liberators we only 3,000 yards from British troops. The 453rd Bomb Group received heavy flak, and the hydraulic system of "Hollywood and Vine" was damaged, resulting in the collapse of the landing gear upon landing and roll out on the runway. This caused further damage to the left wing and two engines, putting the plane out of service until repairs were made. The crew was uninjured, and given a 10-day leave in Scotland, which Robert greatly enjoyed.

Robert's group was ordered to bomb targets near Paris on July 28, but due to heavy cloud cover over France, was unable to do so. Another group of 111 Liberators set out the same day to attack Brussels but was also unable to complete the mission due to weather. Although the Paris targets were not attacked, the squadron was fired upon and received flak. When Allied bombs were not released on a mission over the intended targets, procedure was to drop them into the English Channel upon return. The risk of bringing unexploded ordnance back to base was too great.

Robert flew his final, 35th mission in the B-24 named "The Spirit of Notre Dame," coming full circle, as he had flown his first mission in the aircraft named "Notre Dame." The Spirit of Notre Dame joined with a force of more than 650 Eighth Air Force heavy bombers attacking targets in Ludwigshafen, Stuttgart, and Karlsruhe. The Karlsruhe marshalling yards (a marshalling yard is the area of a railroad yard where railroad cars are linked together) were heavily attacked, and the bombers received moderate flak, but faced no enemy fighters. For the final time, Robert returned to base, having completed his combat tour of duty.

Robert's combat duty was completed, but of course, the war was not. He was transferred to another air base in England, and his new assignment was guarding the payroll office all night armed with a Thompson sub-machine gun. A large amount of money was stored in the office, as all the men received pay in cash. A few weeks later, Robert boarded the troop ship Mauretania in Liverpool for the voyage back to New York City. His fellow passengers were mainly English brides who had married American soldiers and been invited to live with their husband's families back in the United States. After a week of sailing, Robert viewed the Statue of Liberty for the first time, as the ship arrived in New York Harbor.

The servicemen were sent to Fort Dix, New Jersey, for processing from overseas duty, and then transferred to Camp Shelby, Mississippi. After further processing, Robert was given a month's leave and took the train with his Army-provided ticket from Hattiesburg to home at White Castle. At the end of the month, Robert, a loyal Louisiana State University football fan, did not want to miss the Saturday night game, so he caught a commercial flight back to Miami rather than take the return train earlier.

The Army Air Force still had plans for Robert, and he was given a Miami hotel room and more pre- processing mental and physical exams. His superiors wanted Robert to become an aerial gunnery instructor, but Robert wanted a job where he would be doing something more active, so he pretended to know less about machine guns than he did. Soon, he was placed into the newly developed B-32 "Dominator" bomber training program for flight engineers. The B-32 was the last heavy United States bomber produced during the war, developed as a backup to the B-29 "Superfortress." Very little combat was seen by the B-32 before the European front of the war ended, and Robert's unit was cut from training. When the news broke in

America of the war ending, people excitedly celebrated in the streets. Robert was sent to an Oklahoma City air depot where B-29 engines were rebuilt, and enjoyed his return to working normal business hours. The many civilian women employed at the plant were very pleasant, allowing Robert to join the recreational organization at no cost. Everyone enjoyed dances, watermelon parties and swimming.

The greatest excitement in America was the announcement of victory over Japan. Wild celebrations took place in the packed streets, similar to "New Orleans at Mardi Gras," Robert recalled. Robert also said, "The general sentiment in the American population then, was the bombings of Hiroshima and Nagasaki were necessary, because they quickly ended a long-lasting war." It was felt that an invasion of Japan would have resulted in a much greater loss of life.

At war's end, Robert was assigned to a small Kansas airfield, where new planes were being delivered and stored on base, nose to tail, wingtip to wingtip. His job was to remove parts from aircraft. The base had a capacity for thousands of men, but only a few hundred working there, which made for pleasant, relaxed conditions. With extra money allocated, the cook would provide luxury food, such as steak and ice cream, when the rest of the country was under rationing.

At this time, millions of service men and women were discharged, using a points system to determine the order, accounting for the number of service years and amount of combat duty. The persons with the highest number of points exited first. Robert's high point number enabled him to be discharged in six weeks. He reported to the Eighth Air Force Headquarters in Shreveport, Louisiana, and on October 5, 1945, was officially separated from the Army Air Force.

Back at home, Robert worked in a sugar company plant as a

chemist, then at his former position at the state Public Works department, before returning to LSU as a civil engineering student in spring of 1946. He married, and is the father of four daughters. After graduation, he accepted a position

Robert 2012, with photo of self from War Years.

as a civil engineer for the Baton Rouge Public Works Department. After the passing of his first wife, he remarried.

He reflected on his European flying experience as a "most unusual and dangerous experience," adding "I'm glad I did it, but wouldn't want to again!" Robert later served as president of the Second Air Division Association, an organization promoting education about the war, reunions, and friendship. After decades of existence, the organization was disbanded in December 2012. This author enjoyed attending the final reunion in 2012 in Chicago, Illinois.

To learn more, Robert highly recommends visiting the Second Air Division Memorial Library at the Norfolk and Norwich Millennium Library in England. The library was dedicated on November 7, 2001, and the building is England's busiest public library. Her Majesty, Queen Elizabeth, and Prince Philip attended the official opening on July 18, 2002. At the 10-year anniversary party for the library, held on November 16, 2011, Robert, as president of the Second Air Division Association, cut the ceremonial cake. The Library is located in the Forum Building in the center of Norwich, with a lending collection of more than 4,000 books covering all aspects of

American life and culture, and is a living memorial to nearly 7,000 Americans in the Second Air Division of the US 8th Army Air Force who lost their lives. Museum web site: www.2ndair.org.uk for further information.

The Museum of the Air Force at Wright-Patterson AFB, Ohio, near Dayton, is one location where you may see a B-24D on display. Go to www.nationalmuseum.af.mil on the Web.

CHAPTER 2

If you can read this, thank a teacher. If you can read this in
English, thank a veteran"
- (author unknown)
"To a World War Two veteran, these words say it all."
- George Snook

During my frequent visits to the state of Ohio as an airline
crewmember, I immediately noticed the particularly strong
patriotism and conservative nature of the citizens there. On
national holidays and other days of remembrance, a generous
amount of American flags are always on display, and Memorial
Day parades attract large crowds.

One day, while driving in the Urbana area in west-central
Ohio, my husband Mark and I stopped at Grimes Field, a self-
supporting general aviation airport, with a 4,400 foot asphalt
runway, flight school, cafe, and a museum. The Champaign
Aviation Museum is the home of the B-17 Flying Fortress
"Champaign Lady" restoration, a decade long project that has
attracted hundreds of volunteers, aviation enthusiasts and
veterans. (The museum, and how to become involved, is
discussed in the afterword.)

One special man we met, a volunteer on the B-17 project,
was George Snook, a veteran of 30 missions over Europe as a
flight engineer and gunner on a B-24, a member of the 703rd

Bomb Squadron, 445th Bomb Group, based at Tibenham, England. The squadron commander at Tibenham at that time was the Academy Award-winning actor, James M. ("Jimmy") Stewart, then an Army Air Force major.

Left George Snook. Right George Snook 2013

Snook was raised in Ashland, Ohio, south of Cleveland, one of seven children. He recalls "never being hungry" during the Depression because the family grew a large garden. He recalled, "We brought in 20 bushels of potatoes in the fall, and Mother canned everything in sight. Chickens provided eggs, and we only had to buy flour, salt, and sugar."

Snook took a job at A. L. Garber, a printing company. As the clouds of war gathered over Europe in 1940, Snook's brother entered the service. Snook drove a friend who wanted to join the Army Air Force to Dayton, and the next week, applied himself. The Air Force informed him there would be an opening in two weeks. Upon returning home, Snook learned that he had just been drafted.

Snook joined 65 other recruits, all wearing overcoats, at the Erie Depot (railroad station) bound for Columbus to receive their uniforms, "the most ill-fitting things I had ever seen in my life." He underwent basic training Camp Atterbury, Indiana, and before Snook was finished, he was informed there would be an opening for flight engineer school at a later time. In the interim, he attended a four-month aircraft mechanics school run by civilians in Lincoln, Nebraska. Naturally mechanically inclined, Snook enjoyed the school and earned good grades. There he worked on P-38s, P-40s and other fighter aircraft.

Next, he was sent to Salt Lake City for assignment, and gunners were needed. "If you attended the school and passed the tests, you received 50 percent more money, and, being in for the short haul, I decided to go for the money," Snook recalled. At Wendover Field, Utah, gunnery school, the recruits were initially trained on small handguns and the old "Springfield" rifle, then worked up to 30 caliber and 50 caliber guns. Snook said the school had excellent instructors and he easily passed the tests. For weekend recreation, they would all be taken by a 2 ½-ton truck to Ely, Nevada, a wide open little city where "everything went." Some of the fellows lined up at the prostitution houses, but Snook said he "did not participate!"

Upon return to Salt Lake City, assignments were made for the formation of aircraft crews. Ten men came together for a B-24 crew. The pilot's name was Captain Williams, from Florida, and the crew all blended together as one team in very short order.

The crew took more training in Pocatello, Idaho, primarily air-to-ground gunnery firing. The men thought it was a nice town, except for the prohibition on liquor sales. Snook asked for a one-time ride in the tiny ball turret under the belly of the plane to see what it was like. On that 90-degree day, Snook stripped off his shirt and was dropped down into the turret. The

turret rotated 360 degrees and was effective at shooting ground targets, but there was no room to wear a parachute, and the man in that position had to depend on the men above to be brought back up into the

George Snook top right with his crew. body of the aircraft. Later, when Snook served as flight engineer, he sat in the upper turret, crawling into position after takeoff. It was very exposed up there; the enemy had a good, clear shot at you, and the turret made him feel very isolated from the airplane.

One day, the pilot asked the men, "Have you been up through Yellowstone?" All the men said no, so they toured the park by air, and all agreed it was quite a sight.

Upon completion of training, orders were received for three crews to report to Sioux City, Iowa, the demarcation center, to replace three other crews who had crashed on training flights. Pilot error, usually not mechanical error, caused training flight crashes, which were not uncommon. The crew wondered where they would be going, and there they also met their squadron commander, Maj. James M. Stewart. Soon, they were issued machetes and assumed they would be going to a southern destination. They picked up a B-24 named "Hap Hazard" at Lincoln, Nebraska, and flew it to Morris Field, Florida, near West Palm Beach.

Captain Williams, the pilot from Florida, decided he wanted to perform a low fly-over of his house in the Coral Gables area. He put the airplane in a shallow dive, whereupon Snook tapped him on the shoulder and said, "Mac, this is not a fighter, and when you pull back on the stick, it is not going to respond immediately." Williams said, "Yes, yes, I KNOW, George!" and pulled up in plenty of time. Snook recalled, "When I flew, I was responsible as the flight engineer to bring it back in one piece, and I let them know it!"

New recruits waiting at Ashland, Ohio train station.

The flight to England with a 10-man crew and five military passengers took 13 days, and stops were made at Puerto Rico, British Guiana, Brazil, and Dakar, Africa, where a new base had been built with a steel runway with mats to land on. At the next stop in Marrakech ,Morocco, Snook and the airmen noticed the large disparity between the "haves and the have not's," seeing young women and children sift through the garbage, taking scraps of meat, bread, and whatever they could eat.

The men then arrived over England, approaching from the west, to avoid the fighting over France. The pilot and navigator then disagreed on the airplane's position, and with only 15 minutes of fuel remaining, they spotted a base, called in a mayday, and landed there. A few other B-24s, under the same predicament, landed at that base also. The crews spent the night, and the next day flew 20 minutes over to Tibenham, arriving just before Thanksgiving.

**7-4-1944 Presentations
445th Bomb Group**

The Tibenham base commander was Col. Robert H. Terrill. The colonel was a particularly experienced pilot, accumulating over 5,000 hours of flight time, and Snook said he was an "excellent, excellent, B-24 man - he knew how to handle that bird!" The colonel also had been the base commander at Sioux City, and rode over to England on Snook's flight. (Terrill retired in 1964 as a lieutenant general, with a distinguished career that included pioneering and improving the efficacy of offset radar bombing. During the Korean action, he maintained a high state of training and effective mission capability for stateside B-50 bases; and he introduced new tactics over Korea reducing attrition without loss of bombing effectiveness. As director of operations at the Strategic Air Command at Offutt AFB, Nebraska, he implemented new tactics and means for controlling and launching the entire SAC force, and held other distinguished positions before retiring.)

Snook's first (and routine) combat flight was a mission to Kiel, Germany, on December 12-13, 1943. At that time, Allied fighters would escort the bombers to the English Channel and salute goodbye, as that was all the fuel capacity the fighters had. There was no protection from fighter escorts until about Snook's 12th mission in early 1944. After the fighters were outfitted with belly fuel tanks, they could provide escort for the bombers for the entire mission and return to base.

On this first mission, Snook began a habit of careful preflight inspections. Part of the inspection involved crawling out on the wing through a hatch in the upper turret to check the security of the fuel cap. Caps were secured by a piece of copper wire attached to a post, and Snook carefully ensured that on every airplane he served as a crew member, the proper amount of fuel for each mission was securely carried.

George Snook asked Jimmy Stewart to pose for him.

Was Snook ever nervous about going on a mission? "No, at that age, you do not think about mortality," he said. "Even today, youngsters think the same as we did, that you will live forever. Being afraid to fly was not in our vocabulary." Weather was never just cause to cancel a scheduled takeoff for a mission, even when visibility was down to nothing. But the time between each aircraft's departure would be increased from 30 seconds to one minute.

Snook's 13th mission on February 25, 1944, to Nuremburg, Germany was quite dramatic. After coming off a target, procedure dictated that pilots drop 500 feet in altitude to gain speed to leave the target area as expeditiously as possible. The aircraft took an unexploded 88 millimeter shell, which traveled past the radio operator, hit the armor plate on the rear of the pilot's seat, traveled down through the bomb bay door, and blew a large hole in the port side of the airplane, large enough to stick one's head out. The waist gunner watched as Snook's parachute and shoes flew out the hole. Once the aircraft reached a lower altitude, Snook removed his oxygen mask, and with the screwdriver and pair of pliers he always carried, checked the damage. After determining that the hydraulic lines to the landing gear were shot out, and also communicating with the waist gunner was impossible, Snook used his pliers to pinch all the hydraulic lines he possibly could to maintain accumulated pressure to assist in the operation of flaps and brakes. The main wheels were manually extended by 25 turns of a hand crank in the top of the bulkhead. Crew members could verify the main gear was down and locked was by observing metal yellow blocks falling into place at the same time. Snook crawled up into the nose where the nose wheel, a huge wheel, was located, and crawled underneath it and pushed it out. There was also a metal block for a visual confirmation of the nose wheel being down and locked, but the wheel would not lock. Once weight is applied to any unlocked wheel, it is expected to collapse.

In an emergency, the radio operator fires a red flare, which ensures preferential treatment for landing. Just prior to landing back at base, the pilot ordered everyone except Snook to sit in the tail as counter weights. Snook stood between the pilot and co-pilot to call out airspeeds so the pilots could watch the runway and concentrate on the landing. The pilot held the control wheel back, so the airplane rode on the main landing gear and tail skidded. The nose wheel held until they turned off the runway and stopped. Maj. Jimmy Stewart had been flying the lead airplane that day, and met them right away to ensure the crew was all right. He never left the flight line until all of his crews were accounted for. There was a saying during the war, "If you walked away, it was a good landing," and Snook and the crew walked away.

Snook flew with Stewart on maintenance test flights, but not in combat. Stewart was a bit older than most of the pilots, a well -respected, down-to-earth, natural leader, who led many bombing missions over Germany. At one point, pilots were reporting a high rate of mechanical problems with the aircraft, and it was getting out of hand. So Stewart and Snook began to meet aircraft arriving back to base, and would take them up for a test flight themselves. They did not want aircraft unnecessarily sitting on the ground.

George Snook wearing flight jacket commemorating his aircraft.

On the B-24, the No. 3 engine was always started first, providing electrical power, enabling the auxiliary power to be shut down. One day, the pilot reported, "No electrical power to any of the engines." So Stewart and Snook started all the engines. There was still no electrical power, and the ammeters all read zero. There was a regulator unit underneath the cockpit with identical gauges having adjustments for the power, and Snook recalled, "Someone had screwed all the taps down to zero, preventing any electrical power from being generated, so I adjusted them back to the normal position, and then went back up to the cockpit and informed Stewart everything was now working correctly. What Stewart did with that crew, I'll never know, but I imagine there were severe consequences for the deliberate tampering of the airplane."

Photos of B-24s in the early part of the war showed the nose-turrets blocked out, because they were considered top-secret. After the Germans captured a few of the aircraft, the U.S. top brass didn't care about blocking out photographs anymore. The turrets were converted from stationary to rotating around 1943.

After completing the required 30 combat missions, many of the men went stateside to train on B-29s for missions over Japan. Snook and the radio operator in his crew, Frank Mangan, elected to remain in England in June 1944, as they preferred not to get involved in another theater. In the interim, Snook accepted flight engineer instructor status.

George Snook salutes in front of Champaign Aviation Museum, Urbana, Ohio 2013.

The operations major asked for two men to run the Non-Commissioned Officers, (NCO) club, a comfortable bar in a nice building, and Snook and Mangan accepted the task. They found the "till" and the storage room empty, and within a month, the slot machine operation funded all the beer and scotch the men could drink. Soft drinks were delivered, and beer came in barrels. The scotch was bought from a distiller in London, and they hired bartenders, a bookkeeper, and cleaners. Featured were many dances, attended by the girls of Norwich, and many of them became wives of the servicemen, as they were eager to leave England to go stateside. The club operated until the end of the war. The two men went to London with the some of the leftover funds, bought liquor for $3 to $5 a bottle, and sold it back to the men at base, to the men's delight, for 50 cents a bottle. The Red Cross also had been very good to the men, so the rest of the leftover funds were donated to the organization.

George Snook salutes in front of Old Glory and B 24 photograph, Urbana, Ohio 2013.

Snook was informed that he would be flying home. At Prestwick, Scotland, crews of five were formed in war-weary B24s, 10 passengers were placed aboard, and they flew the northern route home, landing first in Bangor, Maine. The men were elated to see American pine trees, and again consume domestic beer, milkshakes and hamburgers. There was never fresh fruit in England during the war, as it was too expensive to ship, and although they ate canned fruit there, it was not the same.

The men went home for two weeks leave, then returned to Camp Atterbury. Snook had valuable instructor, flight engineer and gunner experience, and the military wanted to retain him for the time being, in case he was needed. In the meantime, he and some of the men were sent for rest and relaxation to Miami Beach, Florida, by train. They were given a lower class of accommodation than their tickets showed, and at Louisville, Kentucky, they exited the train, stayed at the Brown Hotel, and the next day boarded another train to Miami Beach with the right accommodations. They enjoyed 30 days in Florida.

In 1945, Snook was sent to Liberal, Kansas, where his superiors wanted him to become a B-24 engineer instructor. Snook observed the green crews being readied for training, and didn't feel he could do it anymore, as he had completed 30 combat missions, and flown the equivalent of halfway around the world. He asked the flight surgeon to ground him, and then worked on the flight line. The war was then over in Europe, and soon, also in Japan. Snook felt gratitude to President Truman for authorizing the dropping the atomic bombs on Japan, ending the war sooner. At war's end, "More whiskey came out of trunks than I have ever seen in my life," Snook said. The next day, he asked to be discharged, with just under three years of service.

Upon returning home, Snook worked for a printing company on a four-color offset press, then accepted a position selling Frigidaire and Westinghouse appliances for the Ohio Public Service Electric Company, later bought by Ohio Edison. In 1973, the company went out of the appliance business, and Snook worked in the marketing division, in Springfield, Ohio, until his retirement in 1985. He and his wife, Barbara, raised four children and in retirement remained very active in the community.

Website for the 445th Bomb Group: www.445bg.org

The Jimmy Stewart Museum may be visited at 835 Philadelphia Street, Indiana, Pennsylvania. See www.jimmy.org for more information.

CHAPTER 3

"Nature arms each man with some faculty which enables him
to do easily some feat impossible to any other"
                                        - Ralph Waldo Emerson

Arthur "Art" L. Kemp, also a regular volunteer on the B-17
project at Grimes Field, Urbana, Ohio, was a B-17 tail gunner
and veteran of 35 missions over Germany and France. Visitors
to the airfield can view his uniform and other artifacts on
display in the hangar museum. He came perilously close to
losing his life during the war.

A native of Sidney, Ohio, Kemp was drafted, joining the
Army Air Force on February 25, 1943. After training at several
air bases in Florida and Illinois, he left for overseas duty in June
1944, reporting to Polebrook, England, as a member of the
351st Bomb Group, 508th Squadron. Drafted personnel were
assigned a serial number beginning with "35;" volunteers'
numbers began with a "1" and officers' a "0."

Kemp flew most of his missions serving as tail-gunner, twice
as a waist gunner and once as a top turret gunner for "green"
crews who needed an experienced gunner in those positions.
Surprisingly, each gunner's hearing was not too badly affected,
as they wore earphones built into a tight helmet. Over the
helmet the gunners wore a large steel helmet, called a "beanie
hat," (similar to a professional baseball player's helmet),

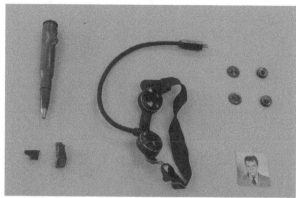

50 caliber shell, pieces of flack, throat microphone, coat button
compasses, civilian ID photo if ever caught on the ground.

Fur lined boots, throat microphone, oxygen mask & WW II Mae West
life vest from Art Kemp collection.

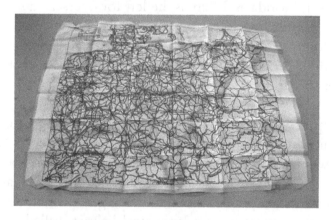

Silk map of Europe carried by all airmen.

deflecting about 90 percent of the incoming flak.

Most of the time, the greatest danger came not from direct fire, Kemp recalled, but massive amounts of flak moving through the air. The crew learned quickly to discern the type of flak fired by the Germans. The 88 millimeter shells generated black smoke, the 105 millimeter shell smoke looked red, and the 155 millimeter shells appeared white. The 155s had sharp-edged grooves cut in them and exploded at a range of 40,000 to 50,000 feet. The incoming flak underneath the aircraft was the most dangerous, as the pieces continued their upward trajectory through the aircraft. The 88s were always shot four at a time in steps, and procedure dictated a crew member would quickly call the pilot so that the airplane could move out of the line of four shots.

Art Kemp Champaign Aviation Museum Urbana, Ohio 2013.

On most missions, Kemp was the tail gunner in the lead aircraft. "One felt more secure and safe, flying in that position," he said. Kemp's third mission began with a 2:30 am wake-up call. After a 3:30 am breakfast, the mission briefing began, and the target of Crepy, France was announced. After taking heavy flak in previous missions to Berlin, Germany, and Rouen, France, this mission did not sound very intimidating.

The crew left base and reached their "bombs away" point

without any incident. After dropping their bomb load without a scratch, the group prepared to turn back to base. Fifteen minutes later, the group entered a heavy pocket of flak, and from his position in the tail, Kemp could not see exploding flak burst gravely wounding the pilot. A piece of flak entered near the pilot's ankle, continued through his leg, and exited at the knee. Blood poured from his knee, soon rendering him unconscious. The co-pilot, announced over the intercom, "Don't worry boys, I'll get you home!" However, he had never previously landed a B-17.

Art Kemp holding medals and airman photo from the war.

Five hours later, as the airplane reached Polebrook, flares were released over the field, standard procedure to let the ground crew know there was someone wounded aboard. Just as the co-pilot set the airplane in position for landing, the pilot regained consciousness, landed the airplane, then slumped back down into his seat. After parking the plane, Kemp and his fellow crew members anxiously waited to see if their pilot would live. The medics gave the pilot seven blood transfusions, and removed his boot. Kemp's stomach turned, as a large amount of bright red blood poured out of the overturned boot. After 45 minutes, the medics stabilized the pilot, removed him from the pilot's seat, and rushed him to the hospital.

A few days later, Kemp rode a bicycle across base to visit his pilot, and was surprised to find him lying in bed, a medal pinned to his chest.

Art Kemp, left, and George Snook, right at B-17 restoration project, Urbana, Ohio 2013.

The morning of Kemp's 11th mission, July 28, 1944, the usual rituals of an early breakfast and briefing were completed, and the guns inspected and cleaned in troughs of solution. After running cloth swabs through the barrels, and wiping down the buffer mechanism, everything was fully wiped dry. The buffer mechanism was adjusted to the mission altitude, to prevent the guns from jamming. The crew donned their flak suits, obtained parachutes and their heated flight suits, and began the mission. As always, Kemp noted the blue exhaust flames shooting downward from the superchargers engaged during the takeoff roll. The target was an oil factory in Merseburg, Germany. What was to come on this mission would never be forgotten by surviving crewmembers the rest of their lives.

After the 351st bomb group formed, they headed east over the English Channel. Kemp and his crew were flying the last aircraft in the last squadron of the last group, the position known as "Tail-End Charlie." This position was especially easy prey for any German fighters attacking from the rear. Shortly thereafter, a Focke-Wulf 190 approached from a 6 o'clock position and fired its guns, the rapid firing looking like a flashing neon sign. Kemp immediately fired his twin 50-caliber machine guns in response to the 190's 20mm rounds. Amazingly, Kemp was not hit, as bullets flew all around his legs and feet, but they mortally wounded the ball turret gunner. More rounds flew, blowing the ball turret assembly to pieces, sending the turret and the gunner falling to earth. The waist gunner was pelted by more exploding rounds, but saved from death by his flak suit. Unable to return fire, he lay wounded in the airplane belly. The B-17 also suffered casualties of its own - engines Nos. 2 and 3 were damaged and then feathered, and the supercharger on engine No. 4 was disabled. The entire right rear fuselage was coated with oil gushing from the right wing oil tanks. The center of the vertical stabilizer had a jagged hole. The crew was in trouble, the situation looking worse by the minute.

The Focke-Wulf fighter had been hit by Kemp, and it was apparent the pilot was not flying the airplane, as it continued a forward approach in a slight dive. The pilot bailed out of his fighter, but his parachute failed to open, and he plunged to his death.

Flying on only one good engine and another engine without a supercharger, and with a loss of oil, the B-17 slowed, lost altitude, and became an easy target for any enemy fighter. A Messerschmitt Bf 109 appeared, and the German pilot decided to take a closer look, joining in on the B-17's right wing. Kemp had his hands ready on the guns. The German took a position where the top turret gunner could not get a shot. The bomber crew could only wait for the German to make a move, as the ball turret was gone, the waist gunner incapacitated, and the German too far forward for Kemp's guns. The co-pilot ordered everyone to stay off the intercom, except for Kemp, so they could immediately converse. After what seemed an eternity, the fighter slowed, lowered its flaps, and moved rearward. The bomber crew thought they were about to be finished.

Kemp, remaining motionless, spotted the fighter out of the corner of his eye, as the fighter continued to a position 45 degrees off Kemp's left side. Knowing that he had one chance for a shot, Kemp quickly swung his guns toward the fighter, and delivered mortal shots that sent the fighter down. The fighter pilot looked toward Kemp, as the fighter descended toward the cloud layer, then the German aircraft suddenly exploded.

Shortly thereafter, a P-51 came along and escorted the B-17 out to the English Channel. Then with fuel low, the P-51 left for the nearest base. The B-17 pilot flew the battered airplane back toward their base, and after dropping flares to indicate wounded on board, the B-17 landed with 1 ½ good engines. The pilot taxied to a large hangar area, where the Glenn Miller Orchestra was to play that evening. A member of the orchestra asked who was on the plane and remarked, "They really got shot up!" At the debriefing, the surviving crew members all had a shot of whiskey. The base captain wanted to have a look at Kemp's guns; the last four inches had turned blue, and bead and bubble metal malformations formed on the tips of the barrels. The captain patted Kemp's back, wished him luck, and ordered him to dispose of the guns.

The crew attended the concert that evening after a good meal. Kemp, exhausted, slowly walked back to his quarters after leaving the concert early, reflecting on a day he would never forget.

Kemp later learned the identity of the Focke-Wulf 190 A-8 pilot whose parachute failed, causing him to plunge to his death. Ernst-Erich Hirschfeld was born in 1918, and at the outbreak of World War II, was serving in a flak regiment. Hirschfeld was transferred to the Luftwaffe, and upon completion of his flight training became a flight instructor. In 1943, he was transferred to the Eastern front, where he shot down a Russian LaGG fighter. He went on to 24 victories in approximately 100 missions, the majority over the Western front, including 12 four-engine bombers, until his last ill-fated mission on July 28, 1944.

CHAPTER 4

"Jedem das Seine" ("To Each His Own")
(The sign over the wrought-iron entrance gate to the
Buchenwald Concentration Camp)

Edward (Ed) Carter-Edwards went to a place of devastating evil during the war. For this Canadian airman to survive incarceration in Buchenwald concentration camp, return from the war and recover to live a normal life and spend years speaking to groups about his experience, is a testament to the strength of his spirit.

That 168 Allied airmen from Canada, the United States, Great Britain, Australia, New Zealand, and Jamaica came to be imprisoned for 3 ½ months in Buchenwald is not well known. My husband and I first set eyes on Carter-Edwards at the United States National Museum of the Air Force, in Dayton, Ohio, in April 2012. We noticed a large group of young Air Force recruits gathered in a circle in the museum entrance hall, intently listening to an older gentleman wearing a band of medals across his dark suit jacket and a Royal Canadian Air Force cap. It was immediately obvious he had a unique and special story. We joined the group of listeners, and learned about one of the most incredible stories of the war.

Carter-Edwards, a native of Hamilton, Ontario, Canada, volunteered for service in the Royal Canadian Air Force on August 17, 1942, at the age of 19. His parents worried about the implications of joining the service, but let their oldest son go. Carter-Edwards felt a duty, as a citizen of a country that was a member of the British Commonwealth, to ward off the advancing "Nazi machine."

As a child, Carter-Edwards enjoyed playing with a device called a "cat's whiskers", a simple radio receiver, popular in the early days of radio. It needed no power source or battery, and ran on power received from radio waves by a long wire antenna. It produced a rather weak sound, and was listened to with sensitive earphones. He loved listening to this small gadget, developed an interest in radio, and, when joining the service, the Air Force granted his request to be a wireless radio operator on a bomber.

Carter-Edwards completed basic training in Toronto, wireless training in Guelph, Ontario, and the required gunnery school in Mossbank, Saskatchewan. Mossbank was home to a RCAF gunnery and training school, training Commonwealth forces during World War II. He passed the Morse code test, an exam where a series of two messages would be played in code, and he had to perceive the differences.

In the fall of 1943, he shipped overseas to England, to the Pershore Training Depot, and was assigned as a crew member on the Handley Page Halifax Bomber. The bomber was one of the four-engine heavy bombers of the Royal Air Force, with a crew of seven, and operated by squadrons of the Royal Canadian Air Force, Royal Air Force, Free French Air Force and Polish forces. As the wireless radio operator, Carter-Edwards sat below the pilot and behind the navigator, separated by a half-width partition. The main job of the wireless operator was to listen at base prior to departure for information on change of wind direction, cloud formations over targets and possibilities of diversionary raids. The operator never transmitted in the air to avoid the Germans picking up the radio signal. Carter-Edwards recalled, "Right off the bat, you were told that you were going into a dangerous environment and could be killed – but at that time, death was far removed from my thoughts."

However, he was fully aware of the dangers of the missions, once he became a member of the squadron. The enlisted men all bunked together;

Carter-Edwards, far right returns from mission.

"When you woke up in the morning, and the bed beside you remained empty, you knew that fellow wasn't coming back," Carter-Edwards said. Two men on his crew were officers who lived separately in officer's quarters. Carter-Edwards felt frustrated that he and the other enlisted men were not allowed to eat, sleep or socialize with the officers, even though the entire crew risked their lives as one team.

On his ninth mission, Carter-Edwards' airplane was involved in a mid-air collision, a very common occurrence, as all their flying was done at night. If there were clouds or any kind of weather, it was difficult to see aircraft flying right beside each other, especially if the moon was less than full. When the crew flying above opened the bomb bay to release their bomb load, the plane below tried to move quickly out of the way, but if not quickly enough, that aircraft could easily be destroyed, or damaged, with holes in the wings and/or fuselage.

On this mission, another bomber flying directly below Carter-Edwards' left wing dropped its bomb load, causing the airplane to immediately climb as a result of losing all the bomb weight. Their starboard wing hit Carter-Edwards' port wing, smashing 10 feet off and also an engine, causing it to catch fire. The pilot put the airplane into a steep dive so the increased airflow would extinguish the fire and ordered the flight to engineer to activate the fire extinguisher to that engine. The fire was extinguished, and the next problem arose, a severe vibration of the propeller. The airplane lost altitude. Furthermore, the "IFF" box (Identification Friend or Foe) was inoperative, as it was powered by the dead engine, so when they arrived at the English coast, the English began to shoot at them. (It was common for German fighters to attempt to sneak into England behind tired Allied bomber boys.) The backup procedure, "Colors of the Day," (colored fired smoke) was used, and they landed.

As Carter-Edwards departed on his 22nd mission, he had no way of knowing that he would never return to his base for the rest of the war. The designated target that night was a railway marshalling yard outside of Paris, a much shorter flight than into Germany's heartland. On June 7, 1944, about 1 a.m., less than 24 hours after the beginning of the D-Day invasion, a German fighter came underneath the Halifax bomber, fired, and set the entire left wing on fire, rendering the airplane unflyable. Carter- Edwards spiraled down to earth by parachute, along with all six of his crew members in sight. Like a vulture, a German Focke-Wulf 190 circled close by, dropping flares to alert ground forces as to the position of the downed fliers.

After landing in the French countryside, Carter-Edwards hid his parachute under a bush, and shortly thereafter he was relieved to find another crew member. Together they ran blindly through the dark until they came to a fork in the path and they were separated. Thinking the man turned right, Carter- Edwards ran in that direction. (Years later, the two men were reunited, and the airman said he had turned left, was picked up by the

French Underground, and was safely hidden until he was liberated in August 1944.)

After another two days of hiding in the woods, motivated by thirst and hunger and the sound of a church bell indicating a village nearby, Carter-Edwards began looking for help. He approached two women, and using his high school French, asked for a piece of bread. The women asked who he was, and when Carter-Edwards said he was a Canadian airman, they gave him permission to sleep in their barn for a week, only bringing him back into the house at night to feed him. Although language was a problem, the family was able to make him understand that they would pass him along to the French Underground, whose members would move him through Spain, a neutral country. Carter-Edwards gave them his escape kit, containing survival aids- small tools, a compass, photographs and currency. After being given a civilian suit, he was passed through by the Underground, on foot, by bicycle, rowboat across the Seine, and train, to an address in Paris. The Underground supplied him with a false French passport under the new name of Edward Cartier. His guides on the Paris Metro train were a young man and woman, who advised him to appear as though he was sleeping while seated. A large, intimidating German soldier was standing in the train car armed with a "potato masher" (a Model 24 Stielhand – granate, a German hand grenade) and a huge firearm. Carter-Edwards finally took the advice to feign sleep, after initially being unable to take his eyes off the massively built man.

As they drew closer to Paris, the young man and woman explained the identification check, telling him to simply show his fake passport they had supplied, and in the event of a problem, they would create a diversion. All went well, and the couple delivered him to a downtown Paris hotel, instructing him to stay a few days, until the next contact arrived.

Several days later, the pre-arranged knock on the door came, and a short man with thick-rimmed glasses who called himself Georges announced that he was going to take Carter-Edwards and three other men to Spain by car. The driver drove quite fast through Paris, stopped at a Gestapo roadblock, got out and walked over to someone of authority, and immediately six or seven of the German military came over to the car and opened the door. The four passengers were forcefully pulled out, thrown to the ground, and severely beaten. A large German soldier jabbed his Luger between Carter-Edwards' eyes, and proceeded to hit him over the head with it. The soldier asked him in well-spoken English, who he was and why he was there. Carter-Edwards replied, "I am a Canadian airman; I demand protection under the Geneva Convention", displaying his dog tags. Ripping off the dog tags the soldier replied, "You're not airmen; you're all spies and saboteurs, and you will be executed as such." The men were classified as "Terrorfliegers", or terror fliers.

It turned out the men had been betrayed by a collaborator named Jacques Desoubrie, a Belgian traitor and a double agent who worked for the Gestapo during during the German occupation of France. He was the illegitimate son of a Belgian doctor, abandoned by his mother and became a drifter. He entered the Gestapo in 1941 and infiltrated various resistance groups, resulting in the arrest and execution of hundreds of people aligned with the Allied forces. The French Underground was never aware of Desoubrie's movements around French homes and hotels where Allied personnel were hiding. Desoubrie was reportedly paid 10,000 French francs for each person he turned in to the Gestapo, and lived very extravagantly, having several mistresses. After the liberation, he fled to Germany, was arrested after being denounced by an ex-mistress, and executed as a collaborationist in December 1949 near Paris.

The men were taken by truck to the Gestapo-run Fresnes Prison in Paris, spending over a month incarcerated there, hearing the moans and groans of people being tortured by the Gestapo and shots ringing out. After being interrogated for three days and threatened with death, there was no more direct abuse, but the men had to deal with fleas, bed-bugs, cockroaches, scarce food and non- existent personal hygiene facilities. At the end of August, as the captives were being assembled in the prison courtyard, Carter-Edwards caught sight of the young couple from the Underground who had helped him, and made eye contact. He expressed with his eyes how very sorry he was that they would suffer the same or worse fate, just for helping the airmen. It was the last time he saw them.

Trucks and buses then transported the prisoners to the Paris railway yard, where they were forced to stand closely packed in cattle cars. The train load included women, children, old men, and political prisoners. The only toilet facility was an open bucket in the center of the car. During the five days in the train, every time the train car rocked, the contents of the bucket would splash the prisoners in the middle. Two small window slits on either side of the car provided outside air.

At one point the train came to a halt in a tunnel that was filling up with smoke. The men and women in the boxcars could not see anything outside, and began to panic, screaming and crying. It became difficult to breathe, and after what seemed an eternity, the train backed out of the tunnel. The prisoners were ordered to get out of the train cars and carry all the soldiers' equipment over to another train to continue the journey.

The prisoners had been ordered not to go near either small window of the boxcar. At another stop, a young French lad ignored the order and placed his hands on the window ledge to draw himself up to have a look. He was promptly shot in the hand, and the guards opened the door asking if anyone had been hurt. The boy held up his bleeding hand, was hauled out and marched a few steps down the track and shot. Two prisoners were ordered to bury him.

Arriving at Buchenwald, the prisoners were greeted by snarling dogs and whip-wielding SS forces. The doors opened, orders were shouted in German, and the inmates were kicked, shoved, and rifle-butted into various separate groups. The slower prisoners were thrown from the boxcar. The camp's lower section was for newcomers; the middle area for people strong enough for forced labor; and the upper section for people to be executed soon or transported elsewhere. Carter-Edwards' group was herded into the lower section, a cobblestone area fenced by barbed wire. The group had to live and sleep there without cover or blankets, rain or shine. Buchenwald was a slave labor camp, not primarily an extermination camp, established on the Ettersberg (Etter Mountain) near Weimar, Germany, about a 7 ½ hour drive from Paris.

At mealtime, the men were given crusts of coarse black bread, partially consisting of sawdust, and a watery, vegetable soup containing bugs, lice and maggots. A guard told Carter-Edwards the diet was designed to intentionally starve a person in three months.

The Allied Forces prisoners organized under a respected Australian airman named Phil Lamason. A squadron leader, he ranked as the senior officer among the 168 airmen, and worked desperately to smuggle out news of their incarceration. In the meantime, the men marched daily in unison throughout the camp, exercised and refused to aid the enemy by being used as a work party. This upset the guards tremendously. The prisoners demanded relocation to a regular POW camp.

Meanwhile, Carter-Edwards had contracted pneumonia and pleurisy, and was taken to a large infirmary hut with wooden shelf-like beds, where he was segregated with the sick and dying. Carter- Edwards recalled, "It smelled of death and defecation, and I was totally out of my mind for about two weeks over the conditions and fever." What saved his life was the action of a French scientist, held in the camp by the Germans to find a solution for typhus, which was rampant. One day, he asked Carter- Edwards to stand up, and he inserted a needle into his back, sucking out most of the fluid clogging his lungs.

Carter-Edwards rotated in and out of the infirmary several times, moving around to many different beds to avoid having the doctors think he was in there too long. The secret underground operating in Buchenwald did this for the Allied airmen. When a patient appeared not to be improving, the doctors would give that person a fatal injection, and the patient's body was taken straight to the crematorium. One day, Carter-Edwards was ordered out of the infirmary to work in the rock quarry, and a young Belgian clerk offered to take his name off the quarry list and put it on the deceased list, again saving his life. Despite the meticulous nature of the Germans, the quarry name list and the infirmary list were never compared.

Carter-Edwards became physically and emotionally ill, but thoughts of leaving the infirmary never came to mind. He began having dreams involving his parents coming to him, having been raised in a very warm, compassionate family. At the same time, he later learned, his mother was constantly praying for him. She would never sign any papers presented to her during the war acknowledging his death as a long-missing airman and refused to give up.

Carter-Edwards estimated he was in and out of that death hut for six weeks before he was turned out, barely able to walk, and realized he was on his own as just another one of the

40,000 human skeletons walking around camp. When a guard walked up to a prisoner, the prisoner had to stand at attention with palms up. Anything resembling a fist brought a rifle butt in the face or a bullet in the stomach. The guards also threw pieces of the prisoners' clothes into the forbidden camp perimeter zone, and ordered them to go after the clothes. If they disobeyed, they were shot. There were 32 different nationalities in the camp, so communication among the general prison population was poor, and many arguments ensued.

On August 24, 1944, the two large camp factories building parts for the V2 rocket were the target of bombing by American B17s, the attack lasting about half an hour. The factory, and the slaves inside, were obliterated, but the inmates, only 200 or 300 yards from the target area, were not injured due to the great accuracy of the American bombing. Leaflets were also dropped, informing the Germans that B-29s would be coming next.

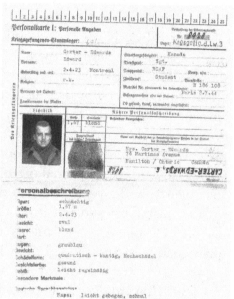

Carter-Edwards on arrival at Stalag Luft III Dec. 1944.

The prisoners strongly felt the shock waves of the falling bombs, and Carter-Edwards and the others, all barefoot, were forced to put fires out and drag out bodies. One day, officers from the Luftwaffe came to the camp to examine the bomb damage done August 24 by the Americans, and an American prisoner from Minnesota who spoke fluent German told them 168 Allied airmen were being held in the camp. The Luftwaffe officers replied that this was no place for fellow fliers. The Luftwaffe did not generally get along with the Gestapo.

The order eventually came for the airmen to be hanged on the meat hooks, a form of extreme torture. A wire would be put around the prisoner's neck, and the wire was hung on the hook until the prisoner expired. Many scratches were dug in the wall, where the suspended prisoners were trying to take the weight off their necks. Lamason wisely withheld the news from the Allied airmen.

About the middle of October 1944, whether through the efforts of Lamason, the scientist in the infirmary, the airman from Minnestota, or someone else, 157 Allied airmen, (excluding Carter- Edwards and 10 others not well enough to travel), were loaded into train boxcars and sent to Stalag Luft III. The boxcars were not crowded, with 30 men assigned to a car with straw on the floor. Carter- Edwards was finally taken out of Buchenwald on November 28, 1944, and on one train stop, some German guards brought him with them into the train station while they got something to eat. The civilians in the station heard that he was a "Terrorflieger" and were preparing to harm him, so the guards returned him to the boxcar.

The conditions at Stalag Luft III were far better, although it was still a prisoner-of-war camp. The men were given extra clothes, the luxury of real showers, and regained some of their strength. (When the men had left Buchenwald, they were given their original clothes back; the photographs taken when they arrived at the camp documented what they were wearing when originally captured.) They were under the protection of the Geneva Convention and received Red Cross packages. For the first time in six months, Carter-Edwards and the other men were able to send telegrams home telling loved ones they were alive. The families at home had suffered great agony during that time, not knowing the fate of their loved ones.

The camp was also the site of the famous "Great Escape," attempted seven months earlier. This resulted in great tension there, as 50 of the Allied officers had been shot after the incident. The airmen were also ordered not to discuss Buchenwald.

The winter of 1944-45 was one of the coldest on record. In January, 1945, the Soviet army was approaching from the east. They arrived at a point 12 miles to the east, and began firing heavy artillery. There were rumors in camp of an evacuation, and one night, between 2 and 3 a.m., with a temperature of 10 degrees Fahrenheit, the men were marched out of camp, allowed to take all they could carry. They were marched north-westward to a camp near Bremen to evade the Soviets, staying there until mid- April 1945. Then the Germans evacuated the camp, and marched the prisoners east, to evade the British. The men, living off the land and sleeping in open fields, were caught in different air attacks by the Allies, who were shooting at and destroying German equipment. "We lost a lot of our boys," Carter- Edwards recalled. As more incoming Allied aircraft were spotted, the prisoners ran into the fields with no opposition from their German guards, and spelled the letters "POW" with their clothing. It worked, the Allied fighters wiggled their wings in acknowledgment, and were more selective in their shooting.

The prisoners found themselves just outside of Lubeck, Germany, on May 5, 1945, when the Allies pushing eastward overran the area with tanks, and that was the end of the war for the prisoners. They stayed in the area for a few days, as celebrations began with shooting guns in the air. Carter-Edwards was unable to join in the celebratory atmosphere. He was so psychologically involved with his experiences in the past year, he couldn't let go. "I couldn't release myself, and I was totally void of anything," he said.

After successful treatment for many months to heal his spirit, he began to return to a normal life and Carter-Edwards was discharged in November 1945. But there was a new, completely unexpected problem. Since he was not Jewish, and had no number tattooed on his arm, no one back home except his own family believed the story of the 168 Allied airmen incarcerated in the Buchenwald concentration camp. A fellow airman, Joe Moser, gave a talk at a Lions Club meeting describing what the men had been through. Afterwards, a man from the audience approached him, and said, "I don't believe a word you said." It was a misconception that only the Jewish people were in concentration camps, as the camps contained many varied groups of people.

Carter-Edwards on the balcony of the Elephant Hotel, Weimar, Germany. On Nov 27, 1927, Hitler held a speech here "announcing a change of course" in the election campaigns.

To this day, military records show very little information about the time the airmen spent in Buchenwald. Carter-Edwards said none of the Allied countries have ever publically acknowledged the presence of the airmen in the camp in 1944.

Carter-Edwards went on to marry, have children, and had a

successful 42 ½-year career working for Westinghouse in Ontario. He has spent decades speaking to audiences about his experience. In July, 2012, he was among 42 Canadian veterans to attend the unveiling in London, England, of a monument commemorating veterans of the Bomber Command. The monument is a memorial to the 125,000 men and women of the Command, almost half of whom did not survive their late-night raids over Germany and Nazi-occupied Europe during World War II. Some 50,000 of those fliers were Canadian, and 10,000 of them were lost: many more originated from New Zealand and Australia, Poland, and Czechoslovakia. The memorial features a bronze sculpture of seven airmen, each nine feet tall. The roof is Canadian, constructed of melted pieces of a Halifax bomber shot down in 1944. The inscription inside honors all the dead of the skies, airman and civilian alike. There, Carter-Edwards met Queen Elizabeth and members of the British royal family at the unveiling.

To learn more, the book, "A Fighter Pilot in Buchenwald: The Joe Moser Story", by Joseph F. Moser and Gerald R. Baron, is available online and at major bookstores. Mike Dorsey directed the film, "The Lost Airmen of Buchenwald" (with executive producers Gerald Baron, Frank Imhof and Duane McNett), featuring interviews with Carter-Edwards, Phil Lamason, Joe Moser and some of the other airmen, telling their harrowing tale. Dorsey's grandfather, E.C. Freeman, was incarcerated at Buchenwald with the other men and survived the war. The film made its debut in July 2011, to a sold-out audience of 1,500 in a Bellingham, Washington theater, who gave a standing ovation.

CHAPTER 5

"Trust in the Lord: To Him I owe it all"-USAF Lt. Col.
(Ret.) Charles I. Williams

It was a great privilege to meet and interview Charles I. Williams, the oldest living Tuskegee airman, just before his passing in September 2013 at age 96. He was disciplined, hard-working, intelligent, highly educated, family-oriented, a civil-rights pioneer and a man of great religious faith.

Williams was born in 1916 in Hagerstown, Maryland, to Silas Roger and Anna Williams, the youngest of three sons. When he was 3 years old, the family moved to Lima, Ohio, principally because in Hagerstown the schools were segregated and in Lima they were not. They traveled by train.

**Captain
Charles I. Williams**

Williams' interest in aviation began in 1927 at the age of 11, when he looked up every day into the sky at the sight and sound of a Ford Tri-Motor airplane on the Chicago-to-Washington mail run. Williams recalled, "I vowed then that I was going to fly." He was also impressed with Charles Lindbergh's flight from New York to Paris in the "Spirit of St. Louis."

After graduating from Lima's Central High School, Williams moved to Los Angeles, California, and found a job working for the famous Louella Parsons, the first American movie columnist, a radio show host, and a gossip columnist. At that time, she was married to her third husband, Los Angeles surgeon Henry "Harry" Watson Martin. Williams lived in an apartment above the garage, and Martin strongly suggested Williams further his education by enrolling in Los Angeles City College. He transferred to the University of California, Los Angeles, in his junior year, majoring in aeronautical engineering, and played football there with Jackie Robinson, who went on to become Major League Baseball's first black player. Williams' junior year at UCLA was interrupted by orders from Washington, D.C. to report to Tuskegee, Alabama, for pilot training. He had been sending applications to the Army Air Force while at the university. "That was about the happiest day of my life," he said. He arrived there in March 1942 and began a rigorous 10-month course. This was possible through the effort of two black civilian pilots, Chauncey Spencer and Dale White, who in 1939 flew a Lincoln-Paige biplane from Chicago to Washington, D.C., to lobby the United States Congress to allow black pilots to be trained in the Civilian Pilot Training Program for the U.S. Army Air Corps. Their efforts eventually paved the way for the "Tuskegee Experiment." "

We flew three different types of airplanes. Training, primarily," Williams said. "We had all white instructors after we left primary. In primary, we were flying a little training plane, a PT-17 trainer, and all the instructors were African-Americans and most of them were from the Tuskegee Institute. We got along fine, but then they had what we used to call 'the washing machine.' A lot of good pilots were washed out of the program for no reason at all." The washing machine "was operated" by white supervisory pilots, who were over the black instructors. "They decided that if they didn't like you or didn't like your color or what you had on, they would wash you out. They didn't take into consideration your abilities," Williams recalled.

Williams completed training in the PT-17, PT-13, AT-6 and P-40 at Tuskegee. From initial training to completing the checkout in the P-40 took about 10 months. Also included in the course were the mechanics of each aircraft. Williams graduated in April 1943, earning his wings as a 2nd lieutenant.

Among the black pilots who successfully completed the program was Daniel "Chappie" James, the first African-American promoted to the rank of an Air Force four-star general. (James retired from the military and died in 1978. Williams, James' first commanding officer, promoted him to 1st lieutenant.)

Williams then reported to Selfridge Field, in Michigan, and practiced maneuvers and formation flying there until January 1944. Williams recalled, "We were finally given orders to go overseas. No one had wanted us because we were black - they thought we couldn't fly. The European newspapers wrote reports stating we were afraid to fly." He reported to Montecorvino Airfield, near Salerno, Italy. The pilots flew P-39s there and stayed about three months. Williams eventually was assigned to Ramitelli Airfield in northeast Italy, near the Alps, home base for 332nd Fighter Group, also known as the "Tuskegee Airmen." The group was assigned P-51s and participated in combat, strafing missions and escorting bombers over Germany, Italy, Czechoslovakia, Poland, and other countries.

One day, Williams was shot down by the Germans over the Italian Alps while on a mission escorting bombers to Czechoslovakia. His engine had caught fire. After parachuting to the ground, he was discovered by an Italian peasant, driving a donkey cart loaded with hay. The two shared no language, so finally, with hand signals, Williams communicated that he was from the Ramitelli Airfield. The Italian agreed to take him there, Williams jumped into the cart under the hay, and they arrived a few days later.

Williams flew his missions in the P39, P47, and P51. The men flew whatever aircraft they were assigned on a particular day. He never lost a bomber he escorted. In May 1945, the group returned home after loyal service risking their lives for the Allied effort, to the "White" and "Colored" signs still present in the United States. One of the men in the squadron talked about returning to Italy because of the continuing segregation back home in the United States.

Ramitelli had a single runway and used area farmhouses as operations buildings. The Tuskegee Airmen used the field until the end of the war. Thereafter, it was used by the 523rd Air Service Group and 949th Air Engineering Squadron. It closed in October 1945, and was dismantled. As of 2012, one former operations and briefing building was still standing.

The Tuskegee Airmen were given the choice of remaining in the military, or getting out. Many left, but Williams stayed for a total of 26 years, flying 101 fighter combat missions with the 332nd fighter Group during World War II and 97 missions in Korea. In 2007, he received the Congressional Gold Medal from President George W. Bush.

In 1949, Williams was sent to Clark Field in the Philippines as a fighter mission pilot on the P51 and F80. Most of the missions were strafing any moving target on the ground. When the Korean War broke out, Williams flew the P51 and F80 out of a base south of Seoul, and returned to the States upon the declaration of the Korean ceasefire. After reaching the rank of lieutenant colonel, he retired from the Air Force. Some of his awards and decorations include the Bronze Star, Distinguished

Flying Cross, Air Medal with four Oak Leaf Clusters and the Congressional Gold Medal, which he donated to the Afro American Museum at Wilberforce, Ohio. As a command pilot he accumulated approximately 8,000 flying hours.

Upon his retirement from the Air Force, Williams opted to resume his civilian life as an engineer at the National Cash Register Corp. in Dayton, where he remained until his retirement in 1981. He married, had a son, and grandchildren.

A friend of Williams said all people can learn an important lesson in dignity from Williams' life: "A lot of times, young people talk about being disrespected, and we see a lot more violence in the community because somebody disrespected them. Here was a man who took far more disrespect back then than our young people have ever seen, and dealt with it with dignity."

You may visit the Tuskegee Airmen National Historical Museum at 6325 West Jefferson Avenue, Detroit, Michigan 48209. See: www.tuskegeeairmennationalmuseum.org

Mr. Ernest Rosser

A certain "synchronicity" often occurs on a project that was meant to be. On one of my road trips for this book, I stopped at a filling station near downtown Springfield, Ohio, and a gentleman pulled up to the next pump, driving a unique and special automobile commemorating the Tuskegee Airmen. Ernest Rosser, a veteran of the trucking business, is the public relations officer for the Ohio Chapter of the Tuskegee Airmen, and has committed much of his free time and energy to speaking to schoolchildren and different organizations all over the country.

Ernest Rosser with his 1965 Dodge Dart
commemorating the Tuskegee Airmen.

1965 Dodge Dart exhaust modification.

1965 Dodge Dart seal.

Interior of Dodge Dart.

Trunk of Dodge Dart.

Painting on Dodge Dart automobile.

His 1965 Dodge Dart automobile features airbrushed paintings of some of the Tuskegee Airmen and their aircraft. Thank you, Mr. Rosser, for your sincere dedication to educating others about the Tuskegee Airmen.

Website for the Tuskegee Airmen, Inc. Ohio Memorial Chapter:
www.tuskegeeairmenomc.com

CHAPTER 6

"Thru Hel'en Hiwater"

Everett Culp proved to be an extraordinarily strong man, having survived a 30-day march across the Austrian and German countryside as a prisoner of the German army. At the age of 91, he recalled bailing out of his B-17 on a mission over Germany, surviving the landing, internment in prisoner of war camps, the "Black March", and liberation.

After graduating from high school, Culp worked across the street from the Dayton, Ohio, airport as a machine operator in a plant that built propellers for the P-39 fighter airplane. He married at age 19; it was "very common for young men to marry their sweetheart before they went to war," he said.

With the war brewing, Culp was interested in becoming a pilot in the Army Air Force. Prior to June 1942, a young man was required to have two years of college to apply to be a pilot, but that requirement was dropped, and then it was a matter of passing a test. The test was heavy in the area of mathematics, which Culp did not enjoy, and he looked for another type of job. He volunteered ahead of the military draft, with the understanding with the draft board he would be assigned to the Army Air Force, not the infantry.

After being accepted in the Army Air Force, Culp was sent to basic training and radio operator school in Chicago, then to

Pyote, Texas, -- "like coyote, but Pyote; they called it the rattlesnake bomber base!" At that time, it was a tiny town with a population of 18. Culp completed second and third phases of flight training at Alexandria, Louisiana, and was established with a full B-17 crew in Kearney, Nebraska, in January 1944. The crew flew the new airplane to Europe via the standard northern route, over Canada, Greenland and Iceland and joined the 303rd Bomb Group at Molesworth, England. With the departure of the 15th Bomb Squadron in 1942, Molesworth was occupied by the B-17 Flying Fortresses of the 358th Bombardment Squadron, the first of four squadrons comprising the 303rd Bombardment Group. The 303rd would remain at Molesworth until shortly after V-E Day in 1945. Culp's first mission was on March 16, 1944. He served on many subsequent successful missions with no incidents or damage. The men had been briefed by a superior, that four things could happen to them

>>They could complete 25 missions, and return home for rest for 30 days ("But don't count on it.")

>> They could be killed.

>> They could be wounded and removed from combat.

>> They could bail out of the airplane and be completely on their own, having nothing except what they carried on their body, including language translation cards, a candy bar, high energy pills, pack of matches, and silk map.

On his 16th mission as radio operator on a B-17 named "Thru Hel'en Hiwater," flying in the No. 5 position in the vicinity of Werl, Germany, the airplane received a direct hit from anti-aircraft fire. Culp had not seen the incoming flak burst from his position, and the fourth burst entered the wing. The No. 1 engine burst into flames, and the entire left wing quickly caught on fire. The fire burst through the fuel tanks, causing an explosion that hit the top-turret gunner and the pilot.

Culp recalled, "I was sitting right behind the explosion,

which made an awful noise." An order was given by the pilot for the crew to bail out. The radio operator sat in the center of the airplane, and his duty before bailing out as the fourth person to jump out the door was to ensure the ball-turret gunner was able to crawl out of the turret, because there was not enough space there to sit with a parachute on. The radio operator was to hand the ball-turret gunner his chute as the gunner exited. Culp looked towards the ball turret, but "there was no airplane section left there."

Carl Culp

Everett Culp

Carlos Culp

Bill Culp

Johnny Culp

Everett Culp and his brothers all served-All returned except for Carlos Culp, who was tragically killed in an accident on VE-Day.

Culp had been thrown into the tail section near the tail wheel from the force of the explosion, just before the tail separated from the fuselage. After disentangling himself from the severed control cables wrapped around him, he stood up and floated out of the airplane at 23,000 feet. He watched the airplane go down, turned over once, saw the sky, turned over a second time, and saw the incoming trees.

At the last minute, prior to the mission, the navigator and bombardier had been substituted out, as they were assigned to crew the lead plane in the next mission. Four crewmembers were killed: the pilot, bombardier, the top-turret gunner, and the tail gunner (who died a day later of injuries from landing on rocks in his partially opened parachute; he sustained a skull fracture).

Drifting down to earth in his parachute, Culp crossed his legs as he was trained in preparation to land in a tall tree. Settling into the tree and attempting to unbuckle his harness, he realized it was a long way down to the water-filled, rocky gulch below.

Just then, two German FW 190s appeared, and Culp wondered if he was going to be shot dead in the tree. One airplane remained in the area of a ridge, the other flew straight towards him. Flying close, the 190 pilot took a photograph and pulled away while waving at Culp, who was left to his own devices, hanging in the tree.

Culp began swinging in the tree from his parachute like a child. Finally he got hold of a branch, unhooked himself, and climbed down from the tree. He spotted the navigator up over a hill.

Culp and the navigator spent that April night in a cold, damp, unfamiliar forest. Sleep was fleeting, as birds chirped loudly all night.

Upon daybreak, the two shivering crew members hoped the rising sun would provide some warmth. Culp found a strong piece of wood to use as a splint so the navigator to drag his wounded leg. Suddenly, two pairs of young eyes peered around a tree, fixated on the men. Two small local children had discovered them, and the men's first thought was, "Uh oh, they will run and get their father!" The children ran away, and the two men found a thick grove of pine trees and buried themselves in pine needles. Barking dogs in the distance apparently sensed the intrusion, but the men were never discovered. After one more night of sleeping in the forest, they began walking.

They reached a river late in the day, and the navigator announced to Culp, "I can't swim!" They then planned to wait until the next break of dawn to walk across a bridge in the early light without company. Just as they neared the bridge, a German military truck drove by. The truck was a mobile dentist unit, and the occupants spotted the two airmen. The navigator, being a young Jewish fellow, was extremely scared and wanted to run, while Culp, feeling weak from not eating for three days, reasoned they would not be able to run very far. At the bridge, the two men raised their hands high in the air. The Germans – the two fellows driving the truck, and the female English-speaking nurse in the rear, turned out to be very kind. Offering the men each a piece of bread and cheese, they informed them they would drive them to the hospital in Essen so the navigator's leg could be examined.

German doctors at the hospital determined the leg was not broken, just swollen from the trauma of the parachute landing. The two men were then taken to the city jail, where Culp had his last sight of the navigator, an officer, because officers and enlisted men were not incarcerated together. As they parted, the navigator sadly recalled how he had been on his 25th mission, expected to be his last, and had a wedding planned, back home.

The next morning Culp and a captured B-24 crewmember, were moved, each having their own guard, to an FW190 fighter base in Dortmund. The German fighter pilots, seeing the American prisoners, gathered around wanting to talk to them. One young German pilot, who spoke excellent English, asked if the men were fighter pilots, and upon learning they were bomber pilots, he was not impressed. The German pilot was only 18. At that time, the Germans badly needed new fighter pilots after suffering heavy losses, and were training very young men for the fast aircraft.

In the middle of the night, Culp was taken to Dusseldorf, then to Frankfurt, where he was checked into a prison camp.

In the interrogation process, there, he realized that the German government had been preparing for the war for years. German spies had been sent to the U.S. before the American involvement to gather intelligence and personnel information. Culp was startled to learn the interrogator knew where he attended high school, worked, and other information. He was also told the tail-gunner had been found after his parachute pulled him over a cliff, forcing a landing at the bottom of the rocky gulch, resulting in a fractured skull and crushed pelvis. The tail-gunner died in the hospital the following day.

The Germans put Culp into solitary confinement, informing him that the lockup would last 10 days. After three, he was released, and interrogated again about his bombing run. Culp consistently gave only his name, rank, and serial number. The Germans would state that the prisoners would be shot, but Culp correctly thought otherwise.

One day, at the Frankfurt camp, Culp asked someone what day it was. The answer: April 30, his 21st birthday! Someone sneaked a cigarette to him, and told him to celebrate.

Culp and many prisoners were ordered to board a train, with 40 men to a boxcar and straw covering the floor. They were not told the destination or how long they would be traveling. Three days later, on May 3, 1944, they arrived at Krems, Austria, at Stalag 17-B prison camp. The men, many sick and wounded, were given a piece of bread and bowl of soup by the Red Cross. Culp took a cold shower, the first one in three months. There was never to be any hot water, but more showers could be taken in warmer weather, although the water was only turned on for two hours in the morning and two in the evening.

Life at the prison camp was dull and monotonous, although the conditions were livable. Four bunks were stacked up in a shelf arrangement, the mattresses were burlap sacks stuffed with wood chips, and each man was issued two blankets. There was no heat, but each man was given an overcoat. The food, Culp recalled, "was whatever we could get – I made up my mind that I was going to eat whatever was offered, unless I thought it was going to kill me." The American government sent clothes for American POWs, and the men received khaki winter clothes and good shoes. They were de-loused every so often.

Some 4,200 American, Russian, French and English prisoners were housed in separate compounds. The prisoners were not allowed to fraternize. Culp could see the Russian compound, which also housed women. There was no difference in the Russian military by sex – one guard said that many of those women were fighter pilots, and one was a tank commander. Throughout the war, the Germans and the Russians bore deep hatred against each other. The Russians housed in camp would die sooner, because they were not given preventative shots and suffered poorer overall treatment. Each morning, bodies of all nationalities would be dumped into a pit.

When new prisoners arrived at camp, the current prisoners would line up to view who was coming in. Culp spotted the left waist gunner and ball turret gunner one day, and waved to them.

In April, 1945, the Russian troops circled Vienna. Culp's camp was only 25 kilometers west of Vienna, and the last thing the Germans wanted was to be captured by the Russians. The German commander issued orders for the prisoners to be marched out, taking only what could be carried on their bodies. The rest of their belongings were to be tossed into a single pile in the middle of the camp compound and burned. At that time, Hitler ordered all prisoners to be executed, but, according to Culp, this German camp commander said, "I will not fulfill that order, we are leaving camp!"

The 4,200 camp prisoners marched west, each with their tin cup and a blanket, covering 15 to 20 miles a day. They lived off the land, digging up potatoes and whatever they could find. They reached the Inns River, near the area where Hitler was born.

Just at that time, General Patton's 13th Armored Division arrived on the other side of the river to rescue the men. They could see the tanks on the other side, but all the bridges had been blown up. For a time, German units in the area were engaging the American tanks in a shooting battle, and Russian troops were also shooting at the Germans. The men heard loud booming sounds all night, Culp recalled. The German troops were just as hungry as the prisoners, and not wanting to be captured by the Russians, many of them abandoned the area and disappeared.

In the morning, an American Army jeep arrived on the road by the river, carrying a captain and three soldiers, and the captain announced they had found a dam down river that had allowed them to cross. He found a German officer, and told him to stand down -- no further firing. The German replied, "You are not going to have any trouble with me," knowing that the war was over at that point, Culp said.

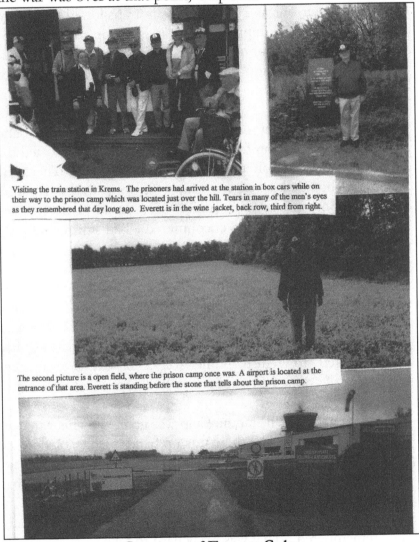

Visiting the train station in Krems. The prisoners had arrived at the station in box cars while on their way to the prison camp which was located just over the hill. Tears in many of the men's eyes as they remembered that day long ago. Everett is in the wine jacket, back row, third from right.

The second picture is a open field, where the prison camp once was. A airport is located at the entrance of that area. Everett is standing before the stone that tells about the prison camp.

Courtesy of Everett Culp

The engineering corps built a pontoon bridge across the river, large enough to hold trucks, and the four- thousand-plus men were picked up and initially transported to a bombed, burned-out German airfield in Bavaria. At the runway, the men were lined up, 25 to a group, to be flown out. They were told not to leave the line for any reason. C47 aircraft arrived, began loading the men and the first flight departed at about 8 a.m. Culp was flown out at 2 p.m. and was transported to Nancy, France, which was equipped with a large camp for "RAMPS" (reclaimed Allied personnel). There, the former prisoners were deloused and given new clothes and good meals. They stayed for several days.

The men were put on a train to Le Havre, France, and arrived at another camp for a short time. A ship transported the Americans and English to Southampton, England. There the Americans boarded a "Liberty Ship", (a troop transport ship), arriving in Boston Harbor in June 1945, after an 11-day voyage. During the voyage, the ship encountered a bad storm, and Culp and many of the men endured seasickness.

After three days in Boston, Culp and other men traveled to Camp Atterbury, Indiana, where they were required to take a course in grammar, table manners, and other social graces before returning to the civilian world. Upon completion, they were released to return home for a 60-day convalescent furlough. Culp took the train back to Bellefontaine, Ohio.

Arriving at the train station, Culp was greeted by his wife and old classmates, but noted there was no band, parade, or flowers. As he got into the car, his wife said, "There is something I want to tell you, before you start the engine. Your brother Carl has been badly wounded, and your brother Carlos was killed in Germany on V-E day" (the same day Culp was liberated). Culp sadly remembered, "That was really hard to take."

After the home furlough, Culp was sent to Miami Beach, Florida, to be re-instated in the Army, and was allowed to bring his wife. The servicemen and their wives were housed in nice hotels with beach access. Culp recalled each meal in the mess hall was 35 cents for the wives.

Beautiful country side in Austria

These are pictures that was taken in the woods where the forced march ended. Everett is sitting by the plaque that tells the history of the area.

The four thousand men that were on the forced march spent five days in these woods. There was a spring by a river at one side of the woods. The men took their tin cups and got drinking water from the spring.

The group of people walking around, remembering the days that they once spent there.

Courtesy of Everett Culp

The war ended, and Culp was discharged at Wright Field, Dayton, Ohio, on September 29, 1945. Culp mentioned, in particular, how families back home suffered while loved ones remained missing. His family was initially informed that he was

71

missing in action. Six weeks passed until they were told he was a POW, the Germans giving the U.S. government the location of Culp's camp. His wife received the first penny post card from him in November, 1944, and he received his reply the next February. Thereafter, a POW was allowed to write two postcards per month home, containing 15 words, and an additional one per month containing 30 words.

Five sons – as well as two daughters -- were born to Culp's parents, John and Lucretia McAdam Culp: John, Everett, twins Carl and Carlos, and Bill. All five served in the military. Carl and Carlos were drafted into the Army together. At age 20, both were wounded in action, three months apart in France. Carl was flown to Southampton, England, to an Army hospital, and later returned to Boston, Massachusetts. From there, he traveled by train to Camp Atterbury, Indiana, to recover in a convalescent hospital, and was discharged from the Army on June 9, 1945. Carlos was accidently killed on VE-Day in his barracks, while his unit cleaned their guns, a terrible shock for the family. He was initially buried in Holland, and later brought back for interment in the family cemetery in Rushsylvania, Ohio.

John Culp was stationed at Camp Gordon, Georgia. Bill Culp joined the Air Force just after high school graduation in 1948, was stationed in Europe during the Berlin Air Lift, and served four years.

Culp returned to Austria with his second wife, Merrilyn, in 1998, to meet with a group of former prisoners of war from Stalag XVII-B. Their bus followed the route of the POW's forced march from Krems to Braunau, Austria. They also visited the site of the prisoner of war camp at Krems, marked by a stone with an inscription about the camp. Tears formed in the eyes of many of the men, as they remembered that time, long ago.

CHAPTER 7

"Trust in the Lord with all your heart; do not depend on your own understanding. Seek His will in all you do, and He will show you which path to take."

- Proverbs 3: 5 - 6

Born in 1919 a South Dakota farming community, Howard "Tommy" Thompson was one of six boys in his small high school graduating class. Three of the boys, including Thompson, went on to become pilots in World War II.

At age 94, Thompson recalled, "Back in South Dakota, we had a nice farm, and every month, a few aircraft would fly by – barnstorming pilots. Charles Lindbergh landed in Iowa at a friend's place. One day, a barnstorming pilot landed in our pasture, and my brothers and I all were given a ride. My older brother was talking with the pilot, and the pilot mentioned having a glider he used to fly, which was towed behind a horse or vehicle to launch it in the air. My brother bought the glider, kept it on the farm, which caused quite a stir among the neighbors. We put it into the air using a Model T Ford, and that was my start in that area. It was a fun farm with six boys in the family. We were allowed to play on Sunday after church, and we would get that little glider flying!"

Thompson went on to college, and in his third year, he enrolled in flying lessons and received his private pilot license.

The country was preparing for war, hundreds of new airfields were being built, so Thompson traveled to Yakutat, Alaska, and was hired to help build runways. He returned home intending to complete his final year of college, but that final year was interrupted by the attack on Pearl Harbor on December 7, 1941. Thompson and three friends went to an Army air base in Minneapolis, Minnesota, and took the entrance exam; Thompson and one friend passed and joined the Army Air Force. They returned home until called to begin training.

"We went through primary training in San Antonio, Texas," Thompson said. "That was a fun time; I really enjoyed it. Upper classmen provided some harassment to try to break you down, to see who could take it. Some of the guys did break down, but I thought it was kind of a fun challenge. Every school had about a 50 percent washout rate.

"Thompson witnessed his first aircraft accident during basic training at the Sikeston, Missouri, airfield, in the southeast part of the state by the Mississippi River. It was winter, and he and another fellow were in flight training, flying solo, lined up for takeoff at the runway. The plane on the runway took off in a reckless fashion, "breaking every rule in the book," Thompson said. (The aircraft in use for primary trainers was the PT 19A Fairchild, with an open cockpit and low wing.) The pilot flew around the pattern, attempted a slow roll, and hit the runway 50 yards ahead of them. After witnessing the crash, Thompson had no desire to fly, but the instructors did not give their students much time to think about it and ordered the student pilots return immediately to the air.

One day at Cape Giardeau, known then as Harris Army Airfield, 40 miles south of Sikeston, (both east of the Mississippi River), another trainee was performing aerobatics with an instructor without having fastened his safety belt. The airplane rolled inverted, and he fell out, to the ground, it was assumed. Years later, Thompson was talking to an underclassmen friend from his senior year who had washed out of training at Cape Giardeau, and commented, "You sure had a bunch of crazy guys down there. One even fell out of his airplane!" The other fellow said, "That was ME! I used a parachute, and fell several thousand feet before landing."

B-25 Pilot Howard (Tommy) Thompson

Soon, Thompson and his group were sent to BT-14 training at Independence, Kansas. This was the only school for these aircraft, which had the same configuration as the AT-6. As he and his classmates were doing calisthenics one day, Thompson saw an airplane spiral down toward the ground. It did not recover, resulting in "another messy event about a hundred yards away," he recalled.

Many of the men became airsick during training, including Thompson. He was offered an "E" (elimination) check ride, an opportunity to fail and be removed from flying, but wanted no part of that. Eventually, he got over the air sickness.

Advanced training took place in Independence, in the At-17 Cessna twin engine fabric airplane, referred to by the men as the "paper bomber," and the Curtiss At-9, a beautiful radial-engine airplane.

In La Junta, Colorado, where the countryside was flat, the men went through advanced training in the B-25. Thompson lost an engine on takeoff on his first solo flight, quickly feathered the propeller on the failed engine, and flew a large, wide circle back towards the field, lining up with the runway. The control tower was a very modest two-story high platform, and the controller would flash a green light to clear the pilots for landing, and a red light signaling a go-around. Thompson received his green light to land, but at the same time another student was approaching from above for landing. The controller frantically pointed a red light at the other student, trying to get him to clear the area, but the student did not comply and continued inbound towards the runway. Not wanting to attempt a go-around on one engine, Thompson simultaneously landed on the grass next to the other student touching down on the runway.

The students were rough on the B-25 aircraft in training, often dropping them 20 or 30 feet onto the runway during landings, wearing out the tires. The very next day, Thompson blew a tire on takeoff, returned for landing, and was able to remain on the runway that time.

In 1943, at Columbia, South Carolina, Thompson received final training on the B-25, joined the 500th Squadron, 345th Bomb Group of the 5th Air Force, and received his full crew with a new airplane just out of the factory. Each pilot had a second pilot who assisted with setting gauges and trim, and other duties. Thompson said one pilot he flew with was just "a little too brave", and he reported the sloppy pilot. The next day the pilot performed a hot-rod takeoff in another aircraft, with three passengers on board. This pilot, the second pilot, and passengers all died when the flight crashed on takeoff, due to improper airspeed control. Thompson said that was hard to take, especially because the pilot had just recently married.

Ten B-25 crews were assigned to overseas replacement, and Thompson and his crew, along with the other crews, ferried their aircraft from Columbia, South Carolina, to Sacramento, California. Thompson enjoyed his crew, and the group of aircraft was assigned to fly to the island of Oahu, in Hawaii. The navigator was from the Air Transport Command – a joint command of US military logistics units in the Pacific Theater of World War II – and expected to be of high quality. The group of aircraft should have all been flying the same heading, but someone was flying two degrees difference, as Thompson and his crew were drifting away from the pack. Thompson asked his navigator to verify the heading, and he replied, "This is my 13th crossing, and I know what I am doing!" They became so lost out over the Pacific Ocean, they were not able to use the low-frequency radio range (LFR) procedure of flying a four- course pattern while listening to certain radio signals to identify specific airways in the sky. Pilots navigated the LFR by listening to a stream of automated "A" and "N" Morse coded. They would steer right, for example, when hearing an "N" stream ("dah-dit, dah-dit..."), to the left when hearing an "A" stream (di-dah, di-dah,..."), and fly straight ahead when hearing a steady tone. Soon, they spotted a B- 24, and realized they were between three and four miles off course. Radio contact was made with Oahu, and the crew was given a heading to fly for landing at base, "a beautiful moment", Thompson recalled. They spotted Diamond Head and landed. "It was the first time I had seen the ocean, and it was a pretty big pond! A very amazing experience for a greenhorn boy from a farm!" Thompson said. The crew flew to three more Pacific Islands on the way to Australia and New Guinea. On the long legs, an extra fuel tank, called a bladder, was carried.

Thompson flew co-pilot for a few missions, then was checked out as first pilot, in the left seat. The Pacific theater flying was especially dangerous, not only because of the aerial combat, but the difficulty of navigation over long distances of water. The casualty rate was very high: Thompson ferried over from the U.S. mainland with 10 crews, and only two of those crews returned. He witnessed many aircraft going down and lost many roommates. Many of the pilots drank to deal with the stress, and sometimes were in no condition to fly a mission the next day. Thompson, not being one to drink alcohol, along with some of his friends, would try to keep busy doing something, such as going down to the beach, gathering anything interesting lying on the sand. At Biak Island, a small Indonesian island just northwest of New Guinea, the men participated in many sports. There was a roughly 100-foot deck built over the ocean, where the men enjoyed relaxing showers.

Howard (Tommy) Thompson, far left, with his B-25 crew.

The missions were rough. Thompson led his squadron on a mission where his wingman aircraft was hit by Japanese fire on takeoff, at the end of the runway. The aircraft caught fire, which spread to the interior, rupturing a gas line. The pilots opened the escape hatch in the cockpit ceiling, and two of the crew members were standing on the back of the pilot's seats, their heads out in the slipstream to get away from the smoke and fire. The shooting continued all around them, while two other aircraft circled in a protective maneuver. The pilot made a beautiful landing on a remote island, and the natives, paddling boats, met them and assisted. A PBY aircraft was sent to pick the crew up, and 45 minutes later, had them out of the area. The co-pilot suffered serious burns to the back of his ears, the two men standing on the seats lived, but two other crew members serving in the rear of the aircraft died after a day or two in the hospital. Thompson, who visited them, recalled the two victims "looked like charcoal."

Flying toward Borneo on another mission, Thompson and his crew flew though some rough weather, using an extra-large amount of fuel en route. Just prior to crossing their target to destroy a large oil tank, one of his own bomb fragments knocked two cylinders off his engine. Another aircraft he was leading headed towards a large bay to make a separate bombing run, burning fuel, when the crew should have made the decision to return to base. Procedure dictated that the lead aircraft wait in the area for the squadron, and all the aircraft were becoming dangerously low on fuel. His squadron, along with another, joined and headed for an alternate airstrip. There was not available fuel for one aircraft to execute a go-around if two aircraft were inbound for the same runway, so Thompson once again landed side by side with a second aircraft, this time a fighter.

"Points" accumulated by each airman were based on the severity of the missions, not the number completed. Thompson was twice given extra recovery time on the ground, due to extra dangerous missions. No counseling was available at that time;

the men were debriefed after each mission and offered a drink. Thompson always refused the drink, participating in prayer instead. He relied on prayer and discipline when good boys died, particularly the day when his radioman, "a young, beautiful, 17-year-old kid flew a mission with another crew, his seventh, and was lost – that was terribly hard.

"One of Thompson's roommates was a survivor of the famous Doolittle Raider mission over Tokyo. Wayne Max Bissell, a native of Vancouver, Washington, was one of the five men on the "Whirling Dervish", the ninth B-25 to take off from the USS Hornet on April 18, 1942. Bissell was the crew's bombardier, dropping three 500-pound demolition bombs and a 500-pound incendiary cluster on targets in Tokyo. The crew then flew 300 miles into China in a storm, and the crew bailed out of their airplane in the middle of the night as it ran out of fuel. Chinese peasants assisted the crew in reaching Allied lines. Bissell went on to flight school and piloted B-25 bombers in the southwest Pacific until his discharge in July 1945. He died January 9, 1997, at the age of 75.

Thompson was shot down once, during an air raid on Manila, Philippines, with an assignment to strike the occupying Japanese installations. One hundred and twenty A20s and B25s took part in the largest air raid in the Pacific theater. Approaching Manila, the crews encountered terrible storms. Sixty aircraft flew abreast, stretching out quite a distance, and Thompson flew on one edge of the pack. Water spouts -- circular air current vortexes extending from the clouds to the water -- were numerous, and had to be avoided, as flying into one is like hitting a wall. Arriving over Manila, Thompson's wingman aircraft was hit on one side, and plowed into a church. Along some of the Philippine airfields, small sheds lined the runway, for one to two miles. A door on each shed dropped down, exposing three or four machine guns, used to fire at the Allied aircraft. The sky was filled with aircraft, Thompson's airplane was not able to gain altitude as they were being fired upon by the ground forces, and one engine was shot and heavily damaged, rendering the hydraulic system operative. The crew thought that was it, but kept hanging on. They considered finding a rice paddy near a jungle, where they could make a shallow water landing and then hide. A P-51, P38, and P40 joined the B-25, as well as a damaged A-20, and they headed for a designated island to attempt a landing. During this time, the co-pilot, flying his first mission, was a nervous wreck, going through three packs of cigarettes. He had just transferred in from completing police work in the Caribbean.

Howard (Tommy) Thompson at home 2013.

The A-20 landed first on the island. A runway was cut into the dirt, and one ambulance was present. It was a bad landing; the airplane spun on the ground and was torn apart. Three of the crew members were seriously injured and were transported by ambulance 40 minutes later.

Thompson called for manual extension of the flaps, due to the inoperative hydraulics. Only the flaps on one wing would extend, so no flaps were ultimately used, and the landing was excellent. Fearing fire the crew immediately opened the emergency escape hatch (it flips up into the air on a B-25), and the four crew members in the front (the co-pilot was the first one out), exited there. The other crewmembers also got out, and again, Thompson appreciated the work of his good crew.

After completing 40 missions, Thompson was called in by the commanding officer, and asked if he wanted to transfer to the Fifth Air Force headquarters in the Philippines to fly more missions. Thompson exercised his option to return home. He married, raised a family, and ran an oil company service.

CHAPTER 8
Requiem For The Fallen

Often, when visiting the headstones or memorials to soldiers or airmen who never returned home, one can miss the impact the death of each individual would have for those who knew and loved him. When visiting a cemetery far from home, this can especially be the case.

At a local level, each individual was a family member and belonged to a community. It is easier to appreciate the loss of a beloved father, son, husband, wife, grandfather, uncle or great-uncle than a faceless service member.

First Lt. Stanley H. "Sammy" Samuelson, and 2nd Lt. Charles "Keith" Kingsley were among those whose final fatal mission followed a period of successful, difficult and distinguished missions. They served on the same B-29 crew on missions in the Saipan-Tokyo area, Samuelson serving as pilot, and Kingsley serving as aircraft navigator. They were part of the 21st Bomber Command, 73rd Bombardment Wing, 500th Bomb Group, 881st Squadron.

Their families have carefully kept their war belongings, letters, and a diary. They were both well- regarded, and deeply loved by their wives and families.

Samuelson, from Medford, Massachusetts, was born in March 1920, to Edwin L. and Florence W. Samuelson. At age 8, after his father died, he lived with his aunt and uncle, Mr. and Mrs. John W. Shields, in Bridgeport, Connecticut. He was a 1939 graduate of Bassick High School in Bridgeport, and the Art School of Pratt Institute in Brooklyn, N.Y., in June 1941. In December 1941, Samuelson enlisted in the Army Air Force and graduated as a second lieutenant from the Columbus, Mississippi, Army Flying School. His first assignment in February 1943 was as first pilot of a B-17 "Flying Fortress" for operations in the North African campaign. On his original aircraft, named "Never Satisfied," flying in the Mediterranean area, he completed 50 combat missions successfully, without a loss of a single crew member. Because of their successes, he and his crew were selected to participate in the August 13, 1943, first bombing of Rome.

Upon returning to the United States on leave, he married Marjorie Stowe, in the Stratford, Connecticut Congregational Church.

Samuelson, by then promoted to 1st lieutenant, was then assigned to a B-29 "Superfortress" Group for Pacific war theater operation, and most of the training was taken at the Walker Army Airfield, Victoria, Kansas. His crew was a smooth operating team, requiring few replacements. In October 1944, he and his crew flew their aircraft to Saipan and participated November 24 in the first raid over Tokyo from that base.

Second Lt. Charles "Keith" Kingsley was born in Celina, Ohio, in March 1916, attended the Celina public schools, where he was a distinguished athlete, and completed three years of pre-medical work at Miami University. He enlisted in the Army Air Corps on January 28, 1943, and received his commission October 23, 1943.

He married Mary K. Hellwarth on March 21, 1944, during stateside leave, and they resided in Kansas until November

1944, when his crew, with Samuelson as the pilot, was assigned to the B-29 base at Saipan.

Samuelson kept a diary, and wrote letters home, and Kingsley also wrote letters home. The following are excerpts from the Samuelson diary and Kingsley's letters to his parents, printed with permission from the families, which allow us to get to know two good men somewhat. The chapter will finish with the story of the loss of the airplane, and most of the crew members, on February 19, 1945.

From the Stanley Samuelson diary:

"On November 5th, our bomber, that we christened "Snafuperfort," was well on her way to the Hawaiian Islands and the coast of California had long disappeared on the horizon. For the first few hours our trip was uneventful, most of the crew asleep or playing cards. Suddenly the plane began to vibrate terribly. One look at the instruments told us that the number four engine was bad, so we had to stop the engine and feather the propeller immediately before she caught on fire. Our co-pilot and I re-trimmed the controls and again clutched in the automatic pilot, which took over the controls and flew the plane for us all the way to Honolulu, on the island of Oahu. The B-29 flies almost as good on three engines as she does on four, however, the safety factor is greatly reduced. The radio operator kept in contact with the ground stations at all times. They kept sending us fixes every 20 minutes showing us approximately our position, just to be on the safe side...

...The following morning, November 6th, the bad engine was inspected, and proven to be absolutely worthless, so we planned on about a two week stay in Oahu. As a rule, all transient crews were restricted to the field. However, due to our expected long stay, the commanding officer gave us permission to go to town and also Waikiki Beach. Everyone took off to the beach with great expectations, only to be very disappointed. There was the beach, not a half mile long, and hardly 50 yards wide. Some of us tried the native surf boards with almost disastrous results. Sure looks easy, but then so does ice-skating. Honolulu is just another large American city; high prices, crowds of people and vehicles running all over the place. The city is filled with Japanese who actually outnumber everyone else on the island. Every time the government tries to draft one of them, they say they are for Japan, and end up in the "clink'...Charley Kingsley and myself loaded up on Kodak film at one of the Navy ship stores...

...On November 13th, our last day on the Hawaiian Islands, I celebrated my first wedding anniversary. I'd have given an awful lot to be with Marge on that day. Never realized I could miss anyone as much as I do my wife...

...Kwajalein, another coral reef, was our next destination. Our plane averaged about 220 miles an hour all the way, and after bucking 12 storms, we finally pulled into the South Pacific Island, ahead of time. Talk about "hell on earth," that was it. The reef looked like the Japs had left yesterday, instead of five or six months ago. There wasn't a whole palm tree on the island. Bullet riddled pill boxes, tanks and landing boats were strewn all over creation...

...Next stop, our home, the Island of Saipan. From the first reports that we had about this place, most of us were pleasantly surprised. Our quarters consisted of semi-circular, steel roof buildings that held about 10 to 20 men. Our ground crews had been here a few months ahead of us, and they did a really grand job of fixing the place up for us ... When we arrived, there were about 100,000 men on the island, and planes stacked up on all the fields ... For the first three days at our permanent base, it rained off and on all day and all night. Leather began to get moldy after the first few days, and most everything took on a musty odor…

…We arrived on Saipan on November 18th. Up until that time, there had been no raids pulled by our group, except a short milk run to Truk. Much talk had been going on as to the coming raid on Tokyo. The "Big Gears" of the B-29 outfits said there were 1,300 pursuits around Tokyo, and we could expect up to 400 attacking us on the first mission.

After five days of being alerted for the coming raid, the weather finally cleared between here and Tokyo, and we were definitely scheduled for the mission on November 24th, Thanksgiving Day. I should say it was Thanksgiving Day back home, and the day after, here, for we are a day ahead of the States…

When I arrived at the plane, everyone was all set to go. Each of our 14 guns had over 500 rounds of 50 caliber ammunition, and the cannon in the tail was loaded and charged. The front bomb bays had extra gas tanks, which made a total to 8,000 gallons of gasoline. Because of the extra gas, our bomb capacity was only 10 500-pound bombs…

…The flight to Japan was uneventful, except that one of our engines started to heat up. Six-and-one-half hours later, we were cruising along at 28,000 feet; very near the Japanese mainland. When the clouds broke, Mt. Fujiyama stood out on the horizon like a beautiful painting done by a master. It was a beautiful sight, and one that very few people will ever witness during this war…

…Soon after leaving Mt. Fujiyama and heading for Tokyo, what we most feared, happened. One of our engines just up and quit on us … Another disappointment – our bomb racks froze and we couldn't get rid of them. By that time our outfit was so far away we gave up all chance of catching them, and commenced looking out for ourselves. It was at this time we blew three exhaust stacks in one engine and she began spitting out flame. To add to our troubles, our bomb doors broke down, and couldn't be retracted…

…Things got hotter than hell, and the guns began to crackle in all directions … Many of the enemy pursuits were hit in some degree or another. All of the gunners were so busy keeping them off, that no one was particular whether he definitely knocked one down or not. This battle, between "Snafuperfort", and 40 Japanese fighters, lasted for almost 30 minutes. We came out without a scratch … Naturally, all of us heaved a sigh of relief when the last fighter turned for home. However, we were far from happy. Our gas was very low, and we still had 1,400 miles to fly over water.

About an hour out from our target, (the engineer) crawled back into the bomb-bay and released the bombs by hand. All the damage we did was to kill a few fish … We nursed our plane home for about seven hours … There was about one hour's gas supply remaining when we finally cut the switches. Two Superfortresses were lost on this first Tokyo raid. One crashed in the harbor at Tokyo after colliding with a fighter, and the other ditched just outside of Saipan after running out of gas. The following morning, all 12 men on this crew were picked up by the air sea rescue. So ended the first mass raid on Tokyo; the battle for Japan proper had really begun in earnest …

…The hospital has been getting a case or two a day of men who have completely cracked, or who were in the first stages. A captain in our squadron, who came over with us, went to pieces when a Japanese plane crashed near him and exploded, about a week ago. Right now, he is on his way back to the States completely finished with flying, after only two weeks on Saipan. Another captain, an airplane commander in our squadron, is also on his way back to the States, suffering from a complete nervous breakdown after two Tokyo missions. Almost everyone here has been on edge lately, and I'm no exception.

Every time the engineers blast the coral on the hill, someone always jumps. Rumors have been going around about the possibility of the Japanese using gas. "Tokyo Rose" said if we didn't stop using our fire bombs, they might start playing with gas. Now, most all of us have one eye on our job, and the other on our gas mask. Three weeks have elapsed since we landed here, and in that time, the enemy has raided us about eight to 10 times ...

December 12th was mission day again. The Mitsibushi aircraft plant at Nagoya, a hundred miles south- west of Tokyo, was the target. We were scheduled for this one, but our plane was again out of commission, so we had to sweat them all out on the ground ... It was late in the evening before we received the final results of the raid. Main target, 40 percent destroyed, and surrounding factories badly damaged. We were all very well pleased with the results, however, it wasn't long before our smiles reversed. Four B-29s were lost ... There is no getting around it; we are all scared and scared plenty.

This stuff of losing crews on every mission is a hard pill to swallow. It wouldn't be quite as bad if our losses were just because of the enemy, however planes ditch out in the middle of the Pacific at night because of engine trouble and other mechanical troubles ...

...There was to be another strike at Tokyo. Take-off happened to be much earlier this time, and at six A.M. we went roaring down the runway, which was hard to see because of rain and darkness. It was impossible to see the other planes, so I flew a pre-arranged course and finally came out of the clouds. By luck, other planes spotted me, and joined on my wing. Kingsley had all the information for the course out, and for a time, it looked as if we were going to lead the whole outfit over Tokyo. A half-hour later, the Colonel's plane finally saw us, and soon they were catching up to take over the lead ...

...Everything looked fine – very little flak and pursuit ... Sorry to say, the luck was with the Japanese, for a bombardier didn't see the target. Instead of continuing on to the secondary target, our Colonel led the group of planes back over Tokyo for a second try. This was unexpected and screwed up the formation. I had to climb to 31,000 feet to keep from ramming other planes. It was on this second run over Tokyo that the whole sky blossomed with ugly flak bursts ... At this time, the lead ship ... led the whole bunch back over Tokyo for the third time ... I was thrown out of formation during the steep turn, so I headed our ship for home...

...We were a few miles off the Japanese mainland when the tail-gunner called into report a crippled B-29 that was following us home. We kept our planes in sight of each other most of the way home for mutual aid in case one of us had to ditch. About seven hours after leaving Japan, good old Saipan showed up on the radar, and we knew we were close to home – once again. During the bull session about the mission the following morning, much was said about the possibilities for improvements in our future raids. One thing is positive – there will be no more second runs over any target...

...It is getting so every combat man lives from one raid until the next. I know that after each mission, I have a new lease on life...

...January 19th was just another mission day. Our B-29 groups hadn't been doing very sharp bombings. This was mainly caused by bad weather over the target. The bomber command was convinced that accurate bombing couldn't be achieved at 31,000 and 32,000 feet, so our outfits had orders to go over at 25,000 feet on this mission. Most all armor plate was removed, plus and extra bomb bay gas tank to lighten the ship on this mission. The target was an aircraft assembly plant west of Nagoya, considered top priority for bombing.

It was (another pilot's) turn to take our plane … About eight hours after takeoff, the planes over the target sent back strike reports by radio. They sounded good! An hour or so after the last B-29 landed, we received all the details of the mission. The primary target was completely destroyed, a number of pursuits were shot down, and all our aircraft returned safely…

…We always look for the Red Cross truck that comes around later in the evening with coffee and doughnuts. It reminds me of my days in Africa when the Red Cross girl came around after each mission…

…It is so very hard living under these circumstances. It's humanly impossible to get used to seeing your buddies go down all the time, so most of us try to ignore the fact…

…Church is really an important part of most of our lives here in Saipan. It is the best feeling I've had here, singing hymns, watching how serious everyone is, and how they listen to every word that is said.."

From the letters of Charles Keith Kingsley:
(All letter envelopes taped on the left side with printing reading, "Opened by U.S. Army Examiner")

10-21-1943 (Stationed at San Marcos, Texas)
Dear Folks, I did it,
I beat the Army and am still here. (Author's note: He had been medically classified as "4F", but it was very important to Kingsley to join and serve his country.) Tomorrow I get a new instructor and I hope to get along OK. I am the only one in the

class who has beat the Army so it makes me feel pretty good. I also did this morning what I have been wanting. I soloed the plane for 20 minutes, landing and takeoffs. It sure is fun to get up there by yourself, everything on your own. It is some feeling to take off and bring it in for the first time. I nearly called you tonight, but thought it would be alright to write as you will find out in only two or three days. I at least have more confidence now, and my new instructor is of the right type I think, and hope I can make it all right...

Love, Keith

10-09-1944 (Stationed at Russell, Kansas)

To: Master Jack Kingsley, of Ohio (his 4-year-old nephew, about to turn 5)

Dear Jack,

How about a letter from your Uncle for your birthday, would you settle for that? No, Jack, I looked all over town, and there was nothing appropriate for a big boy in kindergarten to be found. Hence the letter.

Charles Kingsley on leave holding nephew Jack Kingsley.

How does that school deal go? I bet it is a lot of fun. Mom said you like it because you don't have to take a nap. Is that true, or do you just plain like it?

Here's the proposition. How would you like to have some cash, all your own? No putting it in the bank, just to have when you want it. You see something you want, get it. At your mother's discretion of course. So you will find enclosed, three dollars of your own.

A very Happy Birthday, Jack, and let's see you set all the

candles out in one blow.

Love, Your Uncle and Aunt

10-31-1944 Dear Folks,

...We haven't flown our calibration flight yet, but we expect to soon... You don't need to worry about us while I am gone, as there are 11 of us on the crew, and all will be back. With the crew and plane we have, we can't miss. The way time flies, I'll be back home to spend 30 days leave with you before you know it. None of us are a bit worried, so you needn't either... Love, Keith

11-19-1944

Dear Folks,

...Well, here we are, getting pretty well situated on the island in the Pacific where we are now located... We have our quarters pretty well established. I built a desk and some shelves, but have quite a few things sitting around... Sure do miss you all. Even more here. It seemed when I was in the States, I was practically home, but here, you have a different feeling. Things will work out, so don't worry, at least no more than you have to... Love, Keith

11-30-1944 Dear Folks,

...We were fixing up our Quonset hut today. We cleaned up the front yard, hauled in some dirt, and then leveled it off. We took several coral rocks, and made a border around it. It sure looks different, and much better... I bet that little (niece) Barbara has really changed, as had (nephew) Jackie, no doubt. Probably neither one will know me. Just show them a picture of me once in a while, so they will have some idea. I imagine though, that Jackie will remember... Love, Keith

12-02-1944

Dear Folks

Well, here is what we can now tell. I was in the first one

93

over Tokyo, and it was sure a thrill. We had a little trouble, and got a little behind, so we had more than our share of pursuit. They were sorry, though, as we got one of them. We were pretty proud of it, too. I was quite calm through it all, I was surprised at this, as I really expected to be a little shaky.

We are in Saipan… It is not a bad spot for the hell it has been through. We were swimming and saw "Suicide Cliff," something to be remembered… ("Suicide Cliff" was the site during the last days of the Battle of Saipan where hundreds of Japanese civilians committed suicide by jumping off the cliff.)

…A couple nights later, they came over for a little revenge. Everyone was asleep, and for most, it was the first air raid. I managed to get my helmet, gun, and gas mask, and get my shoes and pants on pretty fast, but by the time I got to the fox hole, they were gone. The next noon … they came back again. This time, I had my shoes on, and got my other equipment pretty fast…

12-04-1944
Dear Folks,
…Today I was paid for last month, and I drew $164.00, at least $100.00 more than I'll possibly spend … We have a pretty nice P.X. set up to get all the essentials one needs. Cigarettes are only five cents per pack… Love, Keith

12-19-1944
Dear Folks,
…I am enclosing a Japanese bill. It is 50 Yen. I got a 10 Yen bill, too. I just got them for souvenirs. I will send one to you, and one to Mary. They are marked with 50 and 10. I am not sure of their value. Before the war, the 10 Yen was worth about $2.80 in our money, and I believe they are similar to our $1.00 and 50 cents… Love, Keith

12-21-1944
Dear Folks,
...I think you get more information from the papers at home, than I can write about. I'll just more or less make a final statement about the raids, then that will suffice, as I really don't see the point in telling all I could. We don't go on all of them, they split them up, and they are darn tough ... Love, Keith

12-28-1944
Dear Folks,
...I was going to write sooner, but Christmas night, the Japanese didn't let us sleep much. They came over and kept us up for three hours, and upset the whole evening's itinerary. It was not too exciting, but interesting. We were able to see one of them shot down by a night fighter...

One of the fellows who goes with one of the nurses, just brought in a clean sheet, and boy, the sweet clean, smell. The nurse got it for him. I think it will be quite a treat to sleep in a bed and sheets. Seems ages since I have, but not so long, either. I just sleep right on the blanket, and cover with the mattress cover, when it's needed... Love, Keith

01-04-1945

Dear Folks,

...To date, we have had five missions, three over Japan, and two short ones. They should give us credit for them, as they were just as hard work, only shorter... Mary just sent me a Kellogg's model plane. If I don't break it cutting it out, I'll sure put it together... Well, folks, I am only sorry I can't write a lot of things so I could make my letters long, occasionally. I will say when they say I can go home. I'll be ready. I wear your silver dollar on every mission, and much of the time on the ground, Dad... Love, Keith

01-07-1945

Dear Folks,

...I have been up to the plane today, doing some work. I aligned the astro compass, and checked the drift meter. The fellows rely on me, and I don't want to fall behind, and let some little thing screw me up ... We have a new plane now, and it sure is a dandy, all of us are quite proud, and have big plans for it. Love, Keith

01-11-1945

Dear Folks,

...I have told all I can in my letters. They are quite strict on what you can write. You can no longer tell where you are, all you can mention is the Marianas. The time difference you mentioned is correct, we are one day ahead of you here... By the way, the mail does seem to be much better. I sure do like to get them. Love, Keith

Keith & Mary Kingsley
Wedding Day

01-22-1945

Dear Folks,

...I am getting to be an old married man, ten months yesterday. Also an old hand at this overseas mission business, the former I want to continue, the latter I don't care much to continue...

I was to church yesterday again, getting quite regular, only miss when we are on a mission, or have something else scheduled. This chaplain is really good. The Catholic chaplain is a sweet fellow, too.

He is up on the strip every mission, and blesses each ship as it pulls up to takeoff position. You see him out there, and it does something to you, all right, and makes you feel much better... Love, Keith

02-01-1945
Dear Folks,
...Saw a very good show tonight, "None But the Lonely Heart," with Cary Grant. They get some really good ones here at times...
The Russians are really going towards Berlin. I wonder how much that will affect this theater of Operations .... I sure hope quite a bit, as it sure seems as though the war has been long... Love, Keith

02-08-1945
Dear Folks,
...We are rationed on our water now. I guess they are waiting for the rainy season. We are allowed five gallons of water per day, per man, for washing, showers, eating and everything...
Our ground school is set up for three out of seven days. Today is supposed to be the last day of the first three. No one feels bad about it either. We all feel that we have enough on our minds... Love, Keith

02-09-1945
Dear Folks,
...They kept us busy today. Ground school this morning, and we flew all afternoon. It really makes a full day. I still can't quite figure how one gets so tired and dirty in an airplane, but you sure do. Then tonight, when we came back, there was no water to shower with, so I had a light wash out of my helmet. It helped though, feel much better now... Love, Keith

02-11-1945
Dear Folks,
...Soon it will be three months that I have been over here. It doesn't seem like it in one way, then in another way, it seems like three years ...
Yesterday, I paid the mainland of

Photo taken over Japan by Charles 'Keith' Kingsley.

Japan another visit. You will read about it, but would no doubt like to know I was in on it... Love, Keith

02-13-1945
Dear Folks,
Evening here, a cool east breeze is blowing in over my desk, a nice warm can of beer is sitting at my elbow, the radio is tuned to "Fibber McGee and Mollie", how does that sound for a set-up...

I am glad you are watching the map. After you get my letters telling I was on a mission, you can figure which one it was, and mark the spot. That way, you will know where I have been. Then, when I get home, I perhaps can tell you something about those you want to know about... Love, Keith

02-17-1945 (Last letter written to his mother and father)
Dear Folks,
...We are starting to paint the inside of the Quonset hut white, it will really look sharp when finished, and much brighter...I spent time piling coral rocks around an area, and making a walk. I'm going to level it off, and find some flower seeds, and pretty up the back yard. Then it will be much better

to look at. I hope I can get some grass started…

That fresh meat once a day is out now for a while. We are back on C-rations and canned stuff. We managed to get filled up, though. We get out the stove, and have a little soup when we get too hungry … How about the job the Navy is doing. Sure hope they keep it up …

Love, Keith

Top Row Standing – Left to Right: Samuelson Pilot, Kingsley Navigator, Wright Bombardier, Shinn Engineer, Martinson Copilot
Bottom Row – Left to Right: Hargrow Tailgunner, Kramer Radio Operator, Weiser Waist Gunner, Goulooze Right Gunner, Janicek Left Gunner, Evans Radar

Two days later, on February 19, 1945, on the crew's seventh mission, their B-29 Superfortress marked Z Square 12 was rammed by a Japanese Ki-45 Toryu fighter plane of the 53rd Sentai, piloted by 2nd Lt. Osamu Hirose, and crashed east of Mt. Fujiyama, on Honshu Island, Japan. Members of the crew were never individually identified, and remains of some of the men were found in the wreckage, and buried in a common grave in a U.S. cemetery near Yokohama, Japan. However, a few of the men were able to parachute out of the burning plane, and were captured by the Japanese. Only one man, Technical Sergeant Robert P. Evans, the radar operator, survived the Japanese camps, and in 1999, met 1st Lt. Samuelson's brother, Edwin L. Samuelson and his nephew, Len Chaloux, at the 24th reunion of the 73rd Bomb Wing Association, and cleared up the mystery of what happened to the crew.

On February 19, 1945, a U.S. Navy-led offensive needed air support from the B-29s. 1st Lt. Samuelson's crew was briefed for a mission over Tokyo. The crew had just flown past Iwo Jima and across the line into Japan to get into position for their bomb run. Two Japanese fighter planes pulled up behind the B-29, and the top gunner began firing. It turned out to be a kamikaze attack, and one of the fighter planes intentionally crashed into the much bigger bomber, striking it in the bomb bay area where an extra gas tank had been loaded. The plane blew apart into two sections. Evans was protected by heavy equipment and large sections of steel. When the plane broke in half, he was sucked out, and thrown clear of the falling debris, wearing his parachute.

Evans observed three other parachutes above him, as he fell in what he recalled to be 200 knot winds. He was picked up by the Japanese, and experienced a brutal time as a prisoner of war.

He was eventually released, and returned home. He felt that 1st Lt. Samuelson, along with some of the others, probably never got out of the airplane. The other men who parachuted out of the airplane were presumed to have died in the Japanese prisoner-of-war camps.

1st Lt. Samuelson was remembered by Evans as a good man who kept calm under pressure, was loyal to the crew, and formed close bonds with his men. He was posthumously promoted to the rank of Captain.

On January 28, 1949, the remains of five crewmembers buried in the common grave in Yokohama were re-buried at the Jefferson Barracks National Cemetery, St. Louis, Missouri, with full military rites. If one is in the St. Louis area, and wishes to pay their respects to these heroic men who gave their lives:

Jefferson Barracks National Cemetery, 2900 Sheridan Road, Oakville (St. Louis County), Missouri, USA. Plot: Section 81, Site 320-321

The flat marker reads:

Charles K. Kingsley 1st Lt
Jack S. Martinson 1st Lt
Stanley H. Samuelson CAPT
Elwyn M. Shinn 1st Lt
John J. Wright 2nd Lt
Air Corps
February 19, 1945

The B-29

The B-29 "Superfortress" was designed by Boeing, and was flown primarily by the United States toward the end of World War II and the in the Korean War. It is a four-engine, propeller-driven heavy bomber. The aircraft incorporated many new features, including pressurized and heated crew areas, and guns that could be fired by remote control.

Large Fowler flaps were added to the wing area to increase lift. At the plants in Wichita, Kansas, and in Renton, Washington, Boeing built a total of 2,766 B-29s. The Bell Aircraft Company built an additional 668 in Georgia, and the

Glenn L. Martin Company built 536 in Nebraska. In 1946, production ended. During World War II, the aircraft were used primarily in the Pacific theater. Tokyo was bombed by as many as 1,000 Superfortresses at a time, destroying large parts of the city. On October 6, 1945, the B-29 named the Enola Gay dropped the first atomic bomb on Hiroshima, Japan, followed three days later by the second atomic bomb attack on Nagasaki.

The B-29s were converted for use after the war for other functions, including weather reconnaissance, rescue operations, refueling, and anti-submarine patrol. The aircraft served again in the Korean War.

In September 1960, the last B-29 in squadron use retired from service.

HEADQUARTERS
73d Bombardment Wing
APO #237, % Postmaster
San Francisco, California

26 April 1945

Mr. C A Kingsley
438 East Market Street
Celina, Ohio

Dear Mr. Kingsley:

Your son served in my command as a navigator on one of our B-29's. In the performance of his duties as a soldier of the United States he has been true to the highest ideals of the Service.

On 19 January 1945, his plane did not return from its mission over Japan. To date everything possible has been done to rescue the men missing in action.

I want you to know that I sincerely regret that the exigencies of the Service must cause such heartaches as must now be yours. I personally feel very keenly the absence of the men missing in action, and I humbly extend to you my heartfelt sympathies.

Sincerely,

EMMETT O'DONNELL
Brigadier General, USA
Commanding

2d Lt Charles K Kingsley
0696107

Letter to the parents of Charles (Keith) Kingsley with permission from the Kingsley family.

CHAPTER 9

"They also serve who only stand and wait"

- John Milton

(Originally a poem about going blind. Also interpreted by some as a tribute to the families left behind, waiting for their loved ones to return from war.)

The price of war is unimaginably high, and the toll can stretch for years. Wars generate no unwounded soldiers. We rejoice when our loved ones return home alive, and grieve when they return in a flag- draped coffin. Often we let ourselves forget the men and women who return with invisible injuries, and/ or obvious physical ones. We do not appreciate the continuing years of healing, long after the war, or the scars that never go away.

After the end of World War II, Mike Pivarnik never again took for granted the use of his hands and feet.

Pivarnik, the son of Czech immigrants who did not speak English, was raised in Mt. Carmel, Pennsylvania, the anthracite coal region of the state. "Pivo means beer, varnik means cook; in other words a brewer," Pivarnik explained. His parents had minimal education, but, like so many European immigrants of that era, they did have "muscle" and the drive to become good Americans. These immigrants applied their hard work ethic in coal mines, farms, and steel mills and meat factories during the Depression.

Upon graduating from high school in 1935, Pivarnik worked for about five or six years at odd jobs. In 1941, with the war approaching, and the draft imminent, Pivarnik evaluated the situation. Not so interested in joining the Army, he enlisted in the Army Air Corps, in 1941, called the "Brown-Shoe Air Force," due to the russet colored brown shoes worn by the personnel. His folks were apprehensive, realizing their son would be facing dangerous duty, but they accepted his decision.

Upon completion of basic training at Jefferson Barracks in St. Louis, Pivarnik attended a four-month administrative clerical school in Fort Logan, Colorado, eight miles southwest of Denver. He was assigned to work in administration at Keesler Air Force Base at Biloxi, Mississippi. Having mastered the commercial course in high school, which included classes in typing and shorthand, Pivarnik's early assignments matched his talents and skills. During this time, the war had begun with great preparatory activity in the military and commercial sectors. Since there was a shortage of officers in the early stages of the war, the Air Corps held the first Officer Candidate School. Pivarnik subsequently "aced" the entrance exam to OCS.

After 90 days, he became a second lieutenant, and received his commission. He availed himself of all opportunities for learning and advancement. It soon became apparent that he did not possess the necessary talents needed to be a pilot, but he looked promising as a bombardier. He subsequently attended bombardier training in Roswell, New Mexico, practicing by dropping bombs – both real and dummies – all over the desert.

Pivarnik was assembled with a B-24 crew, (389th Bomb Squadron), that was based in England, destined for operations over Germany. His first mission over Frankfurt was uneventful. In the second mission over Berlin, however, the German ground gunners were much more prepared, and the B-24 was badly damaged. On this second mission, in March 1944, flown at an altitude of 25,000 feet, with temperatures in the -25F range, Pivarnik froze in the bomb bay, suffering exceptionally severe frostbite injuries.

Michael Pivarnik 2013

After being flown to a hospital in England, he soon lost all of his fingernails and toenails. Doctors were especially worried about the formation of gangrene that could potentially require amputation of his limbs. Pivarnik recalled that his hands and feet were swollen "like boxing gloves." He was unable to wear shoes of any sort for more than three months, but, thankfully, no amputation was necessary.

He had a lot of company in the hospital. He remembered a few of the soldiers in particular. In the next bed was a young, handsome fellow from Baltimore who had lost a leg below the knee. Alongside him, a B-17 pilot was recovering from a crash landing in Poland: after his aircraft was shot at, it caught fire. During that attack, the tail-gunner's parachute had been ripped to shreds, but there were no extras on board. This B-17 pilot had elected to crash land over Poland, rather than to order the crew to bail out, thus saving the tail-gunner's life. Hundreds of other patients in that hospital had similarly horrific as well as heroic stories to share.

After arduous recuperative months at that hospital in the English countryside, Pivarnik joined a medical evacuation back to the United States to continue his recovery. Lowell Thomas, who was later dubbed the Walter Cronkite of radio," was a radio broadcaster on CBS Radio and NBC Radio for four decades. He owned a large estate in Pawling, New York. As a war effort he loaned this estate to the government to do with as they saw fit. The lavish estate was turned into a convalescent center with a full staff of doctors, nurses and corpsmen who served by helping wounded military personnel during their recovery. It was in this location that Pivarnik continued the long road towards healing.

Pivarnik's doctors tried contrast bath treatments for healing his hands and feet. This consisted of soaking them in extremely hot water, then switching to ice water to stimulate circulation. Unfortunately, the frostbite had been so severe that his capillaries were damaged, causing the restrictive circulation problems he was to suffer for the rest of his life.

During his stay at the Lowell estate, Pivarnik's foot became so infected, it required surgery. On the operating table, his leg was strapped down, and the doctor proceeded to use a scalpel to cut away all the infected area. Pivarnik let loose an unearthly shriek: he had not been properly anesthetized. Immediately the doctor realized what happened. He bellowed a barrage of "choice" words, swept all the instruments off the table and stormed from the room, leaving Pivarnik strapped to the operating table. Eventually he was re-anesthetized and his infection was treated. It took a long time for everything to heal.

After four months he was transferred to Beaumont General

Hospital in El Paso, Texas, where the majority of the patients were from the Army, while only a few were members of the Army Air Corps. El Paso had an Army National Guard Base. Some of the troops from that base had been captured, and forced to march in the infamous Bataan and Corregidor Death Marches. The survivors had been returned to hospitals closest to their hometowns, so many were hospitalized at Beaumont. Pivarnik was able to perform the job of facilitating return of the recovered men to new assignments, based on their skills. In the interest of morale, Pivarnik passed along information to some of the men, as he learned the whereabouts of their surviving buddies.

Eventually Pivarnik's hands and feet healed, and he remained in the Air Force for thirty years. He was assigned to General Curtis LeMay's Strategic Air Command, (SAC), serving on B-29s. "Being pressurized and heated, it was a pleasure to fly after the B-24s," Pivarnik recalled. He completed 35 missions over Korea; he was shot at but never again injured.

Pivarnik's last relocation was Commander of the Air Force R.O.T.C. detachment at Indiana University, during the Vietnam War. One of several student anti-war groups was especially confrontational. These students harassed the cadets constantly. Not only did they jeer and protest, they actually threw eggs at the cadets, splattering their uniforms. Despite this harassment, the cadets were strictly instructed never to respond in any way. When the situation escalated, the cadets had to forgo wearing their uniforms around the campus except for very special occasions.

In November of 1945, Mike Pivarnik married his wife of 62 years. Claire had been a WAVE during the war, working as a decoder. In 1945, she accepted the career of being a military officer's wife. Moving from place to place every few years was difficult, but she managed admirably, even with two children in tow. It was an especially stressful time for her while her husband was in Korea, but Claire remained strong. During his time at Indiana University, she held informal seminars for serious girlfriends and fiancées of the cadets. Claire knew from years of experience just how demanding a role of military wife could be, and she wanted these girls to have an idea of what sort of a life they might expect as military wives.

Upon retiring in 1971, Pivarnik continued his education, not only receiving a degree in Political Science, but also three other graduate degrees, while working at George Washington University. His advice to young people: "Examine and evaluate the advantages of serving in the military. It can be a tremendous opportunity."

CHAPTER 10

"Not to have an adequate air force in the present state of the
world, is to compromise the foundations of national freedom
and independence."

Winston Churchill
House of Commons, March 14, 1933

Personnel possessing a strong background in science and
engineering were vital to the war effort, both in combat and in
logistical support. Civil and hydraulic engineering skills proved
especially valuable. Engineers were rarely able to obtain
adequate supplies, equipment or spare parts. Piers and bridges
were often constructed of empty gasoline drums tied together
with rope to serve as temporary spans. Many engineers were
killed or mutilated in accidents at the fronts.

Some scientific and technical advances invented by engineers
and scientists during the war years include the electron
microscope, high-octane gasoline, the Jeep, Teflon, and
synthetic cortisone. Penicillin had been discovered in 1928 and
was mass-produced during the war for battlefield medicine.

Extensive programs of salvage, conservation and recycling
were introduced to the American public to aid the war effort.
Nylon stockings, used cooking oil, tin foil and metal were some
of the materials that could be converted into parachutes, shells
and explosives. Thousands of razor blades could be turned into

machine guns, and lipstick cases became ammunition cartridges. American ingenuity was fully put to use.

Henry Ford, the great industrialist, implemented his vision of mass production to reach staggering war- time goals. He was inspired by the Japanese attack on Pearl Harbor to begin a tremendous manufacturing effort. A massive plant in Willow Run, Michigan, was built to produce B-24 Liberator bombers on a mile-long assembly line. According to an article, "Henry Ford: Helped Lead American World War II Production Efforts" by Richard Grudens, originally published in the January issue of World War II magazine, techniques were improved to produce one bomber per hour, and Ford built 86,865 aircraft, 57,851 airplane engines and 4,201 military gliders by war's end.

Paul Ross, who served as a B-24 pilot during the war, had a long post-war military career and a keen engineer's mind. Born in Illinois in 1917, he completed college in 1940. When he was hired at the St. Louis plant of Curtis-Wright aircraft later that year, there were 1,000 workers. Two-and-a-half years later when he left, there were 10,000 workers.

Ross worked out on the "floor" and first made the suggestion of interchangeability of parts, impressing his supervisors. A new contract was signed to manufacture a new airplane for the Army Air Force. The plant made some of the smaller airplane parts, gave the project to Ross, and ordered him to make the airplane. Ross asked where the jigs were located, and the foreman informed him to make his own, as there were none available, and he was an engineer. Ross went on to develop the AT-9 twin-engine aircraft, and it became number one in production for the company.

Down the street, other engineers working for a company called McDonnell were building a new aircraft plant and attempted to recruit Ross as an engineer, but that month he was selected for the service, and had to turn them down. The company later became McDonnell Douglas Aircraft.

Paul Ross

Ross joined the Army Air Force, graduating from flight school in 1944. He was sent to Maxwell Army Airfield in Alabama for B-24 pilot training, and in July was sent overseas with his crew. Assigned to the 376th Bomb Group, 512th Squadron, he flew 35 missions. At age 27, he was one of the oldest pilots in the squadron. Ross became an air inspector for the group, checking every early-returning aircraft with a mechanical problem to determine whether mechanical failure or crew failure caused it. He found this to be very interesting work.

During his 35 missions, Ross flew 17 different B-24s, because so many were being rotated in and out for maintenance and repairs. Because of his technical experience, he was usually assigned to fly an aircraft with problems that needed troubleshooting. Often, an aircraft limped home to base. During his missions from July 1944 to April 1945, most every aircraft received heavy flak, tearing them apart. (After the war he spoke with a German engineer, who was able to identify where some of the saved pieces of flak had been manufactured by stamped numbers on them.)

On a first mission, the squadron commander always flew the airplane, and Ross served as co-pilot. Prior to the mission, the crew was briefed on how dangerous the mission was to be, and it always proved to be that way. The flak received on one particular mission cut through some of the aircraft equipment, the airspeed indicator failed, and Ross crawled underneath and behind the instrument panel. He noted the indicator line was broken in half and took a tube out of his "Mae West" life preserver and hooked the line together, thus providing a temporary fix to the indicator. This squadron commander's poor landing tore off the nose wheel, and the crew later learned he was a B-17 pilot with little knowledge of B-24s.

Each mission presented different problems. On another occasion the nose wheel canted and would not retract into the hole, and Ross, using his analytical mind, had a crew member remove a gun barrel from the front turret and use the barrel as a pry bar to straighten the nose wheel. It then retracted normally.

In August 1944, on a mission to Ploesti, Poland (the last raid to Ploesti, not the famous low-level raid), the plane took very heavy flak over the target. The No. 1 engine propeller governor was hit, causing the propeller governor to over-speed. The crew completed their bomb drop and a Tuskegee Airman flying a P-51 arrived and provided escort from Ploesti back toward Italy. After an hour of flight, the cylinders in the problem engine melted, and the propeller flew off the engine, whisking by the Tuskegee Airman but fortunately missing his airplane. They continued the trip back to base flying across Yugoslavia at 10,000 feet, missing more bursts of ground flak. Arriving at base, the crew read their status on the briefing room flight board as "Missing in Action," due to their late arrival.

Fragmentation bombs were packaged in wooden boxes. Anytime an assigned mission included the use of such bombs, the crews would save the boxes and reuse the wood to make floors in the Quonset huts where they lived. Wooden floors in their quarters were considered quite a luxury.

One day, another squadron had a sick crew, and Ross's crew was assigned their airplane for the mission. The airplane was in terrible shape, with three pages of notes in the logbook about items not working properly. Upon the Ross's successful return, the commander of the other squadron said, "You made it! We didn't think you would!"

There was considerable pressure by the top commanders to have the maximum number of aircraft in the air, and Ross flew many aircraft used for maintenance training. The standard briefing for those flights noted that there were many missing parts on the aircraft, but the crew would "make it."

On one mission, more heavy flak damaged the fuel system. Each engine had three self-sealing tanks joined together underneath by a small pipe. While the tanks were able to seal themselves after the damage, the pipe was punctured by the flak and 600 gallons of fuel began to drain out through the bomb bay. The crew members working in the aircraft rear had to carefully use 100 percent oxygen fed to their masks as to not become light-headed from the strong smell of fuel. Fuel does explode upon contact with 100% oxygen, and the crew also had to ensure that they did not get too close to the draining fuel to avoid a catastrophic explosion.

The B-24 doors were difficult to open during missions, as they were constructed of sheet metal activated by small rollers. Each roller was set at a slightly different angle to conform to the shape of the airplane. Sometimes the door failed to open, and a crew would drop their bombs directly through the closed doors. On several missions, Ross was faced with this situation and instructed the flight engineer to kick the bomb bay doors to the open position rather than destroy them. Ross earned the Distinguished Flying Cross for this method used on several missions.

Ross's squadron had one airplane modified with a bullet-proof seat for the pilot consisting of heavy steel framed into the sides, rear and bottom. Thus the pilot would be sitting in a cocoon of heavy steel. The seat had a cushion only about three quarters of an inch thick, and the pilot had to sit on it for eight or more hours on a mission. Painted on the airplane exterior was a small mule looking over his back at the stars, and the aircraft had been giving the name "My Aching Ass!" Ross said, "Some of the nose art was unforgettable!"

On a mission on another airplane without the bullet-proof seat, flak hit the rear of Ross's seat, but missed his body. When he retrieved his parachute later in the airplane, he also found flak in the chute.

One day the tail gunner called up to the cockpit and said, "We have to land! Some flak hit my beer can and I'm out of beer!" Another day during flight, one of the rear gunners called and said, "They shot the shoes off my back!" (The crew wore heated shoes, but tied regular shoes to their backs for walking in case they were shot down.) In both cases, Ross replied, "Tough!"

Prior to takeoff, the crew always recited the Lord's Prayer together.

By December 1944, Ross completed 35 missions. The only personal injury to any crew member during those missions was a piece of flak hitting a navigator's head. The navigator lived to receive a Purple Heart. Ross then worked in maintenance, inspecting incoming damaged airplanes.

In January 1945, Ross joined a British intelligence unit in need of graduate engineers to examine German aircraft so the Allies could learn what new technology was being installed in them. The Germans always booby-trapped their airplanes, and Allied officers would be killed. This British unit had six British officers and six American officers, and he was to replace a lost American officer. Ross recalled, "The booby-trap training was interesting. All the instructors were young fellows because they didn't last very long. One guy dismantled the booby-trap, and other was back at the telephone documenting everything."

He traveled to northern Italy and stayed with the British Service 1st Platoon at the home of an Italian count and countess. This provided Ross the opportunity to eat particularly well. Every night, the British would dress for the meal, and the Americans followed suit. Ross did not drink liquor, so the British personnel would look forward to sitting next to him to have the extra wine he declined. The countess got a kick out of the routine, as she had never met anyone who didn't drink.

After six weeks of training, Ross's group was told their first assignment was to parachute into Germany, pick up a V-1 rocket engine and take it out of the country by hay wagon. A week later, the Allies discovered a large train load of the same type engines in Holland, so the mission for Ross and his group was cancelled. Ross continued with this group until war's end.

Ross's Air Force career lasted another 45 years. In 1945, he was assigned to the Inspector General's Office in the Second Air Force in Colorado Springs, Colorado, to close World War II bases all over the western United States. He recalled "all kinds of shenanigans going on -- I would get a message, 'The commanding officer left yesterday and left with all the office furniture.' I would also get phone calls from the wives of injured personnel who thought their husbands were becoming involved with the nurses!"

All the tools for the Eighth Air Force were sent to Sioux City, Iowa, for auditing. Ross received a call that a company in New York wanted to buy all the tools for $.05/pound. Ross implemented a better idea. These tools were passed out to high school and college shop programs all over the United States.

In 1949, Ross and six other officers were sent to Okinawa, Japan, to prepare for the Korean War. Ross supervised two battalions of aviation engineers to inventory all the aircraft armament (guns), and maintain them in full working order.

The next year, Ross flew a C-46 aircraft from the U.S. to Japan, and became fully qualified on it. His co- pilot, a man nick-named "Buck," was a former Tuskegee Airman, and together, they flew over 400 hours in a year's time.

After a year in Korea, Ross was re-assigned to Greenville, South Carolina, as commander of a squadron of C46s and C119s supplying crews to the Korean War effort. In December, 1953, he flew C119s to France, ferrying parts around the country.

Ross recalled making several trips one summer to bring supplies to Thule Air Base, Greenland, located on the northwest coast, 947 miles from the North Pole. On April 9, 1941, "The Agreement relating to the Defense of Greenland" was signed, allowing the United States to operate military bases in Greenland for as long as there is agreement that a threat to North America exists. The agreement was denounced by the Danish government; Greenland is a Danish territory. After liberation Denmark ratified the treaty under the stipulation that the Danish national flag must be side by side with the U.S. flag on the base. Ross remembered the sun circling overhead for three or four months.

Ross spent one winter in Fairbanks, Alaska, to determine in what cold weather conditions the aircraft could be worked on. It was routine to drop Caterpillar tractors and other heavy equipment from aircraft, using multiple parachutes attached to the equipment. One day, one of the parachutes failed, and a tractor plunged 30 feet into the ground. A request was quickly made to send another one.

Ross went on to work on the missile program at Wright-Patterson A.F.B. and retired in January, 1965. After a rest, and the death of his wife, he returned to Wright as a civilian employee working on three programs for the Vietnam War. In 1985, he retired again and bought a farm, "to keep in shape!" He owned a Piper Cub airplane until 1991.

Paul Ross outlived three wives, and said he owed his longevity to his mother, who passed at 98. In his mid-90s he was still doing his own cooking and needed no prescription drugs. His apartment was immaculately decorated with military memorabilia and family photographs.

CHAPTER 11

"Wherever you go and whatever you do, put your trust in the
Lord, He will see you through."
(Favorite quotation of Mr. Ketcham's)

Gailard T. "Red" Ketcham remembers well the day when he
and his father listened to the radio address by President
Franklin D. Roosevelt announcing the attack by the Japanese on
Pearl Harbor. Just 15 years old, Ketcham was living with his
parents and five siblings in the village of Portersville, Ohio.

Ketcham described his life growing up: "My father owned
and operated an auto repair garage and filling station. He built
the garage the year in 1926, the year I was born, and I grew up
under his study and learned the trade as a mechanic. He was a
wonderful teacher, very patient and always teaching me the right
from wrong way to do things. We did not have electricity in our
area until after the war was over, but we did have natural gas for
lights and heating water. My mother cooked on a wood and coal
burning stove that had an open fireplace to heat the house in
winter. I attended school in a small one- room schoolhouse for
my first three years. We were then sent to a former high school
building two miles away in a neighboring town to finish grades
4 through 8, and then sent to high school nine miles away.

"My father was a veteran of World War I, and through his
stories, I was aware of what war meant. He and four of his

World War I buddies organized Memorial Day programs at the local church and cemetery, beginning in 1922, where several veterans from past wars were buried. Local people provided a small orchestra, and I played a violin as my contribution. There were singing groups and a speaker. After the completion of the program, all the children were assembled behind the church and an honor guard carrying the American flag led a parade through the cemetery. The children placed flowers on each veteran's grave. The parade ended at the site of the marker of the Unknown Soldier. The remaining flowers were placed there, and someone in the background played Taps, and then the services would end."

Ketcham's father, a patriotic man, decided to seek work in a city factory producing materials for the war effort. He traveled to Dayton, Ohio in May 1942, and applied for employment at the Frigidaire division of General Motors located on Taylor Street. After filling out an application, he was asked to wait, and within an hour he was assigned to work the next shift. Housing availability was minimal, and he stayed with a brother for two years until purchasing a house in Dayton. He remained at the factory until November 1945.

Frigidaire was given the contract to build 50-caliber machine guns. During this time they reorganized the factory for greater efficiency. The first line of production came out six weeks ahead of schedule, and original costs were cut by 75 percent by the expertise of their engineers.

The company's second contract included building parts for the B-25 Mitchell bomber, the aircraft used on the April 1942 raid over Tokyo by the Doolittle Raiders. The company had a secret second contract to build the auxiliary fuel tanks used by the 16 planes on that famous mission.

The next contract had the company building aircraft

propellers for the Hamilton Standard Aircraft Company, including blades for the B-17 and B-24 fighter aircraft. Frigidaire also had an exclusive contract to build the B-29 propeller.

Dayton was heavily involved the in the war effort during World War II, which led to a manufacturing boom throughout the city. Theaters, restaurants and stores downtown remained open around the clock to support the workers. At one point, emergency housing was put into place due to a housing shortage in the region. During the war, 1,100 manufacturers called Dayton home.

Gailard (Red) Ketcham

Meanwhile, until Ketcham's father was able to purchase a home in Dayton, the family stayed behind in Portersville and Ketcham became the man of the house. He took any kind of odd job offered, and the family raised a large garden. His 18th birthday was on April 1, 1944, and his parents supported his choice to apply to the military branch of his choice, the Army Air Force. On May 17, 1944, he received his orders to report to Fort Thomas, Kentucky, on June 1, and graduated from high school a week after receiving the orders.

On June 1, Ketcham and his family left their hometown together after a large sendoff party in their back yard the day before hosted by the community. The family would join his father in Dayton, and Ketcham would report for basic training. It was a very emotional time for the entire family. After time in Fort Thomas, Ketcham was sent to Amarillo, Texas, for additional training, then was selected for gunnery school at Kingman, Arizona. Ketcham recalled, "On September 17 after completing basic training, we boarded the train to be trained as aerial gunners on the B-17 Flying Fortress. We took classes on identification of enemy aircraft and were taught to take a 50-caliber machine apart blindfolded and reassemble it again. At the firing range we fired a machine gun at a moving target moving around an oval track. It was over a thousand yards distance to the back side of the track and about 300 yards across the front side, and this taught us how to lead the target to fire accurately. I was assigned to the ball turret gunner position, located on the bottom of the plane. It contained two machine guns, and the turret revolved 360 degrees and elevated the guns 45 degrees up and down...

"I graduated from gunnery school on November 11 and received my crew member wings. I was given until November 30 to report to Avon Park Army Air Base in Florida, giving me time to stop in Dayton to see my family over Thanksgiving...

"My father was working in the Frigidaire factory on the 50-caliber machine guns on whose operation I had just trained, and the foreman invited me to the factory to see their production. What a thrill it was to see how they were made beginning with blank pieces of steel and tubing, and coming off the end of the track as a completed and test-fired machine gun ready for the battle front.

In Florida, Ketcham was assigned to his flight crew and completed training. His group of 52 aircraft crews and 20,000 soldiers boarded the Queen Elizabeth headed for Glasgow, Scotland. They arrived on Easter Sunday, April 1, 1945, his 19th birthday.

"We were loaded onto trucks and taken to the distribution point. The 52 crews were sent out to all the different air bases in England. My crew and five others were assigned to the 306th Bomb Group at Thurleigh Air Base in Bedfordshire, England. My crew was assigned to the 369th Bombardment Squadron. We were ready for our call to combat."

The war was progressing quickly on many of the battlefronts, and the Germans were running out of food, fuel and supplies. The Allies were taking advantage of these problems and because at that point they were not losing many planes, the Allied airmen already there were given the chance to complete their tour of duty of 35 missions. Ketcham's crew was then assigned to assist in keeping the aircraft ready for flight until needed as a replacement crew. On May 8 the Germans surrendered, and this ended the fighting in Europe. Ketcham and his crew were not needed at that point to fly combat missions.

Many changes were taking place, and manpower was needed to insure the surrender treaties were enforced. The 306th Bomb Group was selected to remain in Europe to help with this task, and they transferred from England to Giebelstadt, Germany, in December 1945.

During the European campaign, lack of adequate maps and charts caused serious difficulties for the American ground forces. Accurate maps were desired for fire control, fire direction and terrain feature profiles. Thus, the (initially) top secret project named "Casey Jones" was formed to use bombers to photograph more than 2 million square miles of land. This task was assigned to the 305th and 306th Bombardment Groups to take high-altitude photographs of designated areas so that detailed maps of a scale of 1:25,000 could be drawn from the overlaid mosaics of the picture prints. The objective was to produce accurate maps ideally suited to the needs of the ground forces, and the two groups flew thousands of sorties using tens of thousands of flying hours, completing the flying portion of the project in less than 18 months between June 1945 and December 1946. The two groups flew photography missions over the European continent west of the Russian zone border, North Africa and Iceland.

Standing far left, Gailard (Red) Ketcham with his crew.

Dissimilarities in the American and British mapping systems initially seemed to preclude a joint effort. Eventually the U.S. aircraft were equipped with two cameras: one for the U.S. and one for the British. If the camera assigned to the British mission became inoperative, the Casey Jones crews would have to refly the mission flight line to obtain an "original set" for the British. General Henry H. Arnold decided the B-17s could best provide the most stable platform necessary for precise photography.

Ketcham was selected to be an aerial photographer for these missions and he attended training for the operation and repair of these cameras.

After completion of this training and while the military was making additional preparations for this program, Ketcham was temporarily assigned to another program to provide entertainment to thousands of soldiers and other personnel waiting for their turn to go home. The Special Services who provided entertainment for the troops held a contest among all the air bases located in England. A group of men at each air base was to put together a 15-minute stage show. Ketcham was selected, along with 16 other men, a five¬-piece band, four stage hands and a special services officer, to perform at the Palladium Theater in London in a contest judged by the British Broadcasting Corporation (BBC), and won the contest for the best show. Their reward was being relieved of all normal duties with the order to create a two-hour variety stage show. No matter how silly the act, the group used it to make the audience laugh. Over a four-month run, traveling to hospitals and personnel rest areas in England, France, Germany and Spain (the Rock of Gibraltar area), Ketcham's troupe entertained thousands of men waiting to return home. Ketcham enjoyed the assignment.

It was then time for the aerial photography mapping task, and the 306th Bomb Group packed and formed a convoy to Southampton, England, traveling across the English Channel by ferry boats to Le Havre, France. Assembled in an area called "Camp Wings," the men spent three days there, celebrating Christmas. On December 26, they moved out and continued across France by truck, stopping in Paris. Ketcham and a buddy used the opportunity of a 36-hour layover there to see the sights of the city.

The Group moved on through France and into Germany. They drove through some of the same territory Ketcham's father marched through during World War I, and crossed the Rhine River at the same point as his father, 27 years later.

The truck Ketcham drove was a referred to as the WC-51 weapons carrier, a three-quarter ton truck, manufactured by Dodge. "W" was code for 1941, and "C" for the weight rating. The open cab pickup could be fitted with an optional M24A1 machine gun mount, which bolted across the front of the bed. Ketcham's job in the convoy was to carry the K-rations. The convoy drove 50 minutes and rested 10 minutes each hour. On the final stop before noon, he drove down the entire line of men, passing out lunches. Because these were cold meals, Ketcham decided to set some of the meals on the engine block, punching holes in the containers so the meals wouldn't explode. Some of the men asked him how he was able to warm the meals, and being in a practical joking mood, Ketcham had them set their meals on their engine blocks without mentioning adding holes in the containers. Soon cans of beans exploded all over the manifolds down the convoy line!

Arriving at Giebelstadt, Germany, on New Year's Eve, the men were assigned their quarters. The following week, Ketcham and 25 other men were assigned to return to England to assist moving another air base. His job was operating a forklift to load the packed items onto waiting trucks.

The men returned to Giebelstadt, and on February 14, Ketcham was assigned to Port Lyautey Air Base, Morocco, a naval strip located between the cities of Rabat and Casablanca, to begin his duties as an aerial photographer. Twelve B-17s were based there.

The camera well on the B-17 was located in the radio room underneath the floor, close to the size of a normal bathtub. The camera, place in the well, had a viewfinder about six inches by eight inches with a bubble similar to a level. The job was to hold that viewfinder to keep the bubble within its boundaries while in flight. Ketcham recalled, "You sat there for 30 minutes, not daring to take your eye off of it."

There was also the additional problem of ice forming in our oxygen masks, so one of my buddies would momentarily remove my mask, beat the ice out of it, and fit it back on my face. All the while I never took my eye off the ball."

The aircraft cameras took a picture nine by nine inches, and covered 20 square miles taken from 20,000 feet altitude. The crew consisted of a pilot, co-pilot, navigator, radio operator and two camera operators. Due to the intense work with the cameras, the camera operators traded places every 30 minutes. The long missions ran from sunrise to sunset, and extra fuel tanks located in the bomb bay allowed flights up to 14 hours. Heated ovens were provided to keep food warm in flight.

Gailard (Red) Ketcham with mapping camera.

If clouds were encountered in the area to be photographed, the airplane returned back to base. Ketcham enjoyed those cloudy days; he was allowed to fly the plane from either the pilot's or co-pilot's seat while that pilot napped in the radio room. Sometimes on the return flight, the pilots flew the airplane at 4,000 or 5,000 feet to enjoy the countryside, often flying to the Rock of Gibraltar to view which ships were in port.

One day the crew spotted the USS Missouri, the famous battleship used for the signing of the surrender of Japan on September 2, 1945. Ketcham remembered how a doughnut-shaped cloud always circled the spire of the rock.

After learning his tour of duty was over, Ketcham and his group flew to Istres in southern France and were billeted at Camp Pall Mall awaiting assignment to a ship to sail to New York. On June 2, 1946, they boarded the USS Tufts, and ran into many of the men that they had originally sailed with on the Queen Elizabeth to Europe. A good reunion was had by those aboard ship, with the swapping of many stories.

Upon arriving in New York harbor on June 20, Ketcham greatly appreciated the sight of the Statue of Liberty. The group transported to Camp Kilmer, New Jersey, then to Camp Atterbury, Indiana, where Ketcham was processed for discharge from the Army Air Corps. On the morning of June 20, after being presented his discharge papers, Ketcham returned home to Dayton.

He married, raised a family and retired in 1986 after 35 years of service with General Motors.

Gailard (Red) Ketcham in orginal uniform 2013.

Ketcham related the following story he learned following the war:

"When I was in high school, I had a buddy (a brother of my future brother-in-law) by the name of Edgar Sims, a year older. We lived in towns two miles apart, but attended the same high school and played sports together. The last time I ever saw him was on a double date we shared the night before he joined the service. Sims joined the mountain forces in Italy, and his commander was Robert Dole, (later to become the famous Senator Dole of Kansas). Sims became his radio operator to call in artillery and other support if needed. In a battle against German forces, Sims was fatally shot about 100 feet from Dole. Not knowing for sure if Sims was dead, Dole rushed to drag Sims back to cover, regardless, and received severe wounds in his right shoulder and back." (Note: Dole lapsed in and out of consciousness over the next three years, lost a kidney and the use of his right arm and much of the feeling in his left arm. Initially paralyzed from the neck down, his youth, strength, faith and incredible desire to live contributed to his long life of public service. In his 2005 book, "One Soldier's Story," Dole humbly never wrote in detail about his heroic actions that day.)

Ketcham continued, "Senator Dole was closely involved with the construction of the World War II Veterans Memorial in Washington, D.C. My sister and her husband (Sims' brother) and I sent in donations. They received a kind phone call from Senator Dole inquiring if my brother-in-law was any relation to Eddie Sims. Dole later mailed a copy of his television war documentary to our family."

My Soldier Brother
No doubt we never will forget the day
As all of us stood watching from the door.
The day my brother proudly marched away
To face the many tasks brought on by war.

Then just before he vanished out of sight
He stopped and looked around with one last smile
And raised his hand – saluting – yes, just right
Then turned to face the following long miles.

He took with him the love of all of us
Who hold him near and dear within our hearts.
But wait until he has to go "across"
It is not until then the real pain starts.
The house will seem so empty, 'til the day
Our loving brother can come home to stay.

Pauline Ketcham
Sister of Gailard "Red" Ketcham

CHAPTER 12

"I always hope for peace."

- Clarence G. Stearns

In the spring of 1944, a young lieutenant piloting a B-17 Flying Fortress from the left seat on a mission over Germany dove head first out of the forward bottom left hatch of his airplane at  an altitude of 21,000 feet after it was shot, caught fire and entered a flat spin when the controls burned through. That young officer parachuted to the ground, eventually ended up in a German Stalag POW camp, was liberated, and returned home.

His name was Clarence Grover "Stearnie" Stearns. Born in Rochester, Minnesota, Stearns arrived in Yellowstone National Park in 1941, and worked for the famed photographer Jack Haynes. After being drafted into the

Clarence Stearns

Army, he secured a transfer to the Army Air Corps. In September 1943, he flew a B-17 with his newly assembled crew of nine other men: his co-pilot, navigator, bombardier, radio operator/gunner, engineer/top turret gunner, ball turret gunner, tail gunner and two waist gunners to their base at Grafton-Underwood, Great Britain. They were a part of the 384th Bomb Group.

Clarence Stearns (standing, third from left) with crew after first raid over Berlin.

Beginning his combat missions, he asked his superiors how many of the dangerous missions he would be flying. They responded, "Don't worry about it, you won't make it!" (During World War II, the Army Air Force lost 35,933 aircraft in combat and accidents.)

After flying 25 difficult missions, Stearns was informed that he had to fly at least one more, which would be a raid over

Schweinfurt, Germany, on April 13, 1944. Stearns served as air commander of the entire group. Ten bomb groups of B-17 airplanes, more than 200 total, took part in the raid accompanied by 11 groups of B-24 bombers - another 230 airplanes. Approaching Schweinfurt, in his airplane named "Rum Pot," Stearns observed German fighters assembling ahead and radioed for his P-51 escorts. They were five minutes late. The Germans sometimes distracted and drew away the Allied fighter escorts.

According to the post-operation report: "Immediately after our escort had left for the interception of the enemy fighters, a wave of 15 FW (Focke-Wulf) 190s, grey in color and with a fairly large red square painted on the side of the fuselage, made a head-on attack from a great distance away coming in slightly below and flying directly through and between our Lead and Low squadrons.

These aircraft broke to the right and progressed again ahead of the formation in trail. As they continued across the front of our formation, three additional FW 190s, using the latter as a screen, suddenly broke beneath them and dove again into our Low Squadron. During this attack, the Group Leader and six additional aircraft of our Low Squadron were shot down.

Group lead aircraft was shot down by enemy aircraft at 1350 hours, 21,000 feet, (Stearns). Hits were scored on the #3 right engine which was immediately feathered, and the gas tank and the entire right wing broke into a mass of flames."

The German fighters closed in at 500 mph – so quickly and with such terrific noise that it was difficult to assess what was going on. Flashes of fire were everywhere as bullets and tracers flew by. The right inboard engine took a hit and caught fire. Stearns shut down the engine, but the fire extinguishers were inoperative, and the flames spread quickly. Unable to save the aircraft, he ordered his crew to bail out near the town of Reichelsheim.

His co-pilot was in the habit of flying without his parachute harness, telling others it was too uncomfortable. Stearns had strongly advised him prior to the flight to wear the harness, to no avail, as the co-pilot refused and outranked Stearns. Stearns held the aircraft controls as long as he could, while the co-pilot attempted to locate his harness. As the flight controls burned through, and the airplane entered an uncontrollable flat spin, Stearns dived head first out of the bottom hatch.

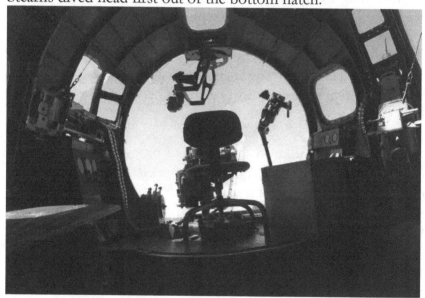

B-17 Bombardier position

The men in the rear of the airplane jumped from the waist door and the bombardier and navigator jumped out of the front escape hatch. A young German boy on the ground saw nine parachutes open, and then a man fall to his death. The co-pilot had elected to escape the fire on the burning aircraft by jumping without time to find his chute.

Stearns elected to free-fall for a time to avoid being detected by ground forces, initially tumbling end- over-end, then rear-end first. The woods suddenly looked very close. He pulled the rip cord, swinging twice, and ended up in a tree. Pulling out of his chute, he ran into the woods, looking for a hiding place. He found a cluster of small trees, crawled underneath, and pulled his flight overalls over his head. The German soldiers shouted when they found his chute, but thinking the chute belonged to the free-falling co-pilot, did not closely examine his hiding area, and moved on. Burying his flight boots in a pile of manure, he took to a road and passed more German soldiers in the dark.

Just before dawn, he entered a village, planning to leave before daylight, but was spotted by a girl who alerted two policemen on bicycles. The policemen assumed Stearns was a forced laborer on the loose and was promptly arrested. Stearns pretended to be "deaf and dumb", hoping the policemen would release him, to no avail. Stearns became a prisoner of war.

He spent the next 13 months in Stalag Luft I, an Air Force POW camp on the coast of the Baltic Sea. Interned there were as many as 8,000 Allied airmen in a meager, boring existence. (The camp Stalag III was the setting for the famous true story of "The Great Escape.") Airmen were limited to seven bed planks apiece to restrict the use of possible tunneling material. Stearns hoped to one day use a treasured miniature compass he had hidden in his mouth during capture in an escape.

He lost 25 pounds as a POW, and food was all that he and the other men could think about during their time in captivity. Rare Red Cross packages held Spam and cigarettes.

After 13 months, the Russians liberated the camp in May 1945, and the Allied POW's worried they were going to be incarcerated in the Soviet Union.(Three days prior to the arrival of the Russians, the German guards abandoned the camp and headed west. The Germans knew they would be shot if captured by the Russians.) Cattle were driven in for consumption, and the prisoners became sick from gorging themselves. A large amount of vodka was also brought in by the Russian troops. After several weeks, Stalag Luft I was evacuated by the 8th Air Force, and Stearns returned to the United States.

Clarence Stearns, 2013, holding a piece of his shot down B-17, given to him after the war.

After the war, Stearns corresponded with a German schoolteacher who was familiar with the location of the crashed airplane. During Stearns' return trip to Germany in the 1980s, the two met in the city of Darmstadt, and the schoolteacher gave him a small piece of the B-17, which Stearns treasured as a memento. The white parachute discarded by Stearns after landing in the German countryside was found by the locals and a young bride used the white material for her wedding dress shortly after the war. The silk parachute material was very scarce in Germany at that time. Stearns kept a photo of the couple displayed in his office.

In June 2013, Stearns, age 93, once again rode in a restored B-17 on a flight over Bozeman, Montana. This came about with the help of the Collings Foundation, founded in 1979 to support "living history" events involving transportation. A foundation plane made a stop in Bozeman, and this author's husband, pilot Mark Cassen, provided air transportation to and from Bozeman from Stearns' Wyoming home.

Clarence Stearns in front of B-17, Bozeman, MT, 2013.

A major focus of the Collings Foundation, based in Stowe, Massachusetts, (www.collingsfoundation.org), has been the "Wings of Freedom Tour" of World War II aircraft, which travels the country with a B-17, B- 24, and P-51 Mustang. The B-17 was the companion of the B-24 in thousands of wartime bombing and reconnaissance missions. Together, they served as the backbone of the US daylight strategic bombing campaign of the war. The Foundation's B-17G flies as "Nine-O-Nine", an 8th Army Air Force, 91st Bomb Group heavy bomber. Their 1944 vintage Consolidated B-24J Liberator, the only one currently flying in the world, flew a record 130 missions over Europe as a member of the 467th Bomb Group. Their P-51C Mustang fighter is named the "Betty Jane."

The Foundation estimates that during 22 years and 2,600 visits to airports across the United States, between 3.5 million to 4 million people have seen these war birds annually. The foundation's two stated goals are appreciation of our freedoms brought about by the sacrifices of our veterans, and to educate young people about our history and heritage. The foundation depends upon private funding from individuals and corporations. A fee is charged for the 30-minute rides to cover operational costs, but for World War II veterans, rides are offered free on an honorary basis.

B-17 cockpit

Stearns said, "I was thrilled to pieces to have the opportunity to ride in the B-17 again. It brought back so many memories and afterthoughts about different missions. I had forgotten how stable the airplane is. When I put my hand on the horizontal stabilizer it was like greeting an old friend I hadn't seen for years."

When asked to summarize his wartime experience, Stearns replied, "Material possessions, money and wealth mean so little. It is your personal relations with family and friends that are most important."

B-17 Bozeman, MT 2013

B-17 Nose Guns, Bozeman, MT 2013

B-17 Tail Gun, Bozeman, MT 2013

Stearns at the waist gun in the
Collings Foundation B-17, 2013.

CHAPTER 13

"Per Ardua Ad Astra"
(Through Adversity to the Stars)
Motto of the Canadian Air Force

Norman Hall, Radar Mechanic, Royal Canadian Air Force.

In his own words:

"I was in my late teens when World War II began. Any fear I had was overcome by the excitement, adventure and chance to begin a life on my own. These are normal teenage thoughts, and when my friends began to join the Canadian military forces, I was tempted to also do so. I had always been fascinated by airplanes, and made flying models. I also learned a lot about electronics by building small radio receivers.

Norman Hall

"A year or so later, a good opportunity arose when the Air Force was looking for radar mechanics. I passed their test and joined the Royal Canadian Air Force as an LAC-Leading Aircraftsman. From my home in Winnipeg, I was initially sent to Toronto to what was referred to as the 'manning pool,' for a medical examination, inoculations and military clothes. I met a few young Americans who had come north to join the Canadian forces.

"After a few weeks of drills, I was sent on leave, then to Halifax, Nova Scotia, to wait for transport by ship to Scotland. A convoy was being formed, and after about a month, I boarded the Pacific and Orient Line, also known as the P&O. While I found out that the ship had a good ventilating system, it had no heat. When we sailed past Iceland, the ship was so cold I slept in my hammock in all my clothes plus a blanket. The trip was uneventful, except for the sound of a few depth charges from escorting destroyers to chase away submarines.

"We arrived at Greenock, just outside of Glasgow. I was surprised to see several black children playing on the docks speaking with a Scottish accent.

"We were put on an overnight train to Portsmouth, on the English Channel. The city had a lot of vacant holiday accommodations to house the men. I enjoyed the warm, sunny weather.

"A week later, they 'sorted us out,' and I was sent to RAF Cranwell, a peacetime training station, in England. There we were given one month of training on the servicing and repair of airborne radar equipment. Then I was sent to an operational squadron on the coast just south of Grimsby, England. The squadrons there were under Coastal Command and equipped with twin-engine Lockheed Hudsons which had been converted into bombers, used against German ships and submarines. They had a limited range and a small bomb load.

"One Hudson had an engine failure after takeoff and crashed just short of the landing strip. It caught fire, and we could do nothing to help the crew due to exploding ammunition and bombs.

"Later I was sent to Benbecula, Outer Hebrides, off the west coast of Scotland. We now had B-17s, much better suited for patrol over the North Atlantic. The only incident there was when one of the planes landed with one wheel up and spun around on the runway.

"I was then sent to Limavady, near Londonderry, Northern Ireland. Our only enemy there was the Irish Republican Army. They would come across the border and try to blow up the aircraft at night. The aircraft were dispersed around the field so it was difficult to guard each one.

"The winter in Limavady was cold and wet. We stayed in Nissen huts and the end wall boards had open spaces between them. One morning, I awoke to find snow on my blanket.

"One interesting break came when I was sent to Malvern, England, near the Welsh border. A group of us were given training on the installation of radar equipment into Lancaster bombers. The long 'Yagi' antennas on the aircraft were used to spot ships, such as the German pocket battleships at the end of Norwegian fjords. A spot or strobe would display on the radar screen, and at night the bomber would fly low over the water to escape the anti-aircraft fire, and aim the aircraft at the ship using the radar display. When the aircraft was at a preset distance from the ship, the bomb was dropped in such a way to skip across the water to the ship. The aircraft turned and climbed before the explosion and maneuvered to avoid anti-aircraft fire.

"After another few weeks, we were sent to an operational squadron where the crews were training on new radar systems. We were then sent back to our own squadron. I never knew if the new systems were a success.

"I should mention that several times I took leave to visit relatives living just north of London. There I heard the 'buzz' bombs flying overhead to hit random targets. Also, I went out one night to watch the anti-aircraft guns firing at German bombers spotted in the searchlights. I soon discovered this was not a good idea when pieces of shrapnel came whistling to the ground all around me. I returned indoors to the protection of a roof. The English roofs were covered with slate, and were fairly durable.

"I was sent to Liverpool to join a large group waiting to board troop ships. I realized we were going to a warmer climate because we were given inoculations for several types of fevers. Soon I was on board one of the ships heading south on the Atlantic. The sea was very rough, but after a few days I found my sea legs, and was able to walk to the ship bow to experience the elevator effect of rising up and down.

"After about a week of travel, I woke up to a quiet ship. I saw a large island in the distance, with the twinkling lights of a town. We were transported to the main dock on landing craft, as our ship was too large. It was tricky reaching the concrete dock due to the heavy swell of the ocean. We made it safely and boarded trucks. We were on the Island of Terceira, in the Azores, in the middle of the North Atlantic Ocean.

"We were taken to an airport belonging to the Portuguese Air Force that had been turned over to the Allies. The grass landing strip was located on a long, narrow valley parallel to the sea. Four small hangars were built into the side of the hill on one side of the strip. After sleeping in one of the hangar concrete floors for several nights, I found it gave me a sore hip. Then I tried sleeping outside, digging a hollow for my hip in the dirt, but found that my blanket was covered with dew in the morning. After a week the pre-fab Nissen huts were erected, and a normal camp was taking shape. We set up our radar servicing in one of the hangars.

"To give the heavy aircraft a metal-covered runway, corrugated, interlocking metal strips were installed over the grass. Our aircraft patrolled that area of the Atlantic Ocean looking for submarines. Things were fairly routine until the Germans changed tactics. When spotted, instead of rushing to submerge, they remained on the surface, shooting at our aircraft. Twice we had to change our radar equipment, covered with blood.

"Our radar officer decided to ride on one of the patrols with the aircrew one night. The airplane never returned.

"Several months later, a United States construction battalion arrived on the island to construct a concrete runway. I later found out why, when I was checking the radar in one of our aircraft. I noticed a number of blips on the screen moving closer. It turned out to be a group of DC-4s, ferrying from the U.S. to North Africa and flown by civilian pilots.

"The island only had one runway, so aircraft had to side-slip to a landing whenever there was a cross- wind.

"Eventually the war in Europe came to an end. I was sent back to England, and then Canada. I was posted to several stations while it was being determined what role Canada would play in the war with Japan. Eventually, I was sent to Sandspit on the Queen Charlotte Islands – across from Prince Rupert – to a PBY-CANSO flying boat station. Our only job was to maintain a small radar beacon.

"When the war with Japan ended, I was given the choice of staying in a peace-time air force, or be discharged. After 4 ½ years in the Royal Canadian Air Force I decided to try my hand at civilian life, and accept a government offer to obtain a university degree in electrical engineering."

Norman married his wife, Pauline, in 1953, and has five children, nine grandchildren and two great- grandchildren. He began his career with the Gatineau Power Company, then transitioned to the federal government as an electrical engineer for the airport lighting systems, working on new runways, approach lighting and standby power systems. In retirement, he and his family have enjoyed their home on a peaceful Canadian lake.

CHAPTER 14

V-J Day: The End of World War II

An aunt of this author served in the United States Navy, working in a medical laboratory in New York City. She wrote this letter to her parents at the end of the war, describing the celebrations. She later married Herbert T. Knight, and was always a kind and thoughtful person.

To: Mr. and Mrs. E. Allan Crowell, Ludlow, MA
From: Hospital Corpsman Ruth E. Crowell
USNRMS, Columbia University, New York, NY
Date: 15 August 1945

Dear Family,
So at last it's happened! Two weeks ago, I would have said it couldn't possibly happen so soon. I had duty last night until 7 P.M. The news was broadcast over a loudspeaker overlooking the square. There was a mob down there watching a baseball game, so the cheering was terrific. For the next half-hour, confetti paper came down in tons all over the city. I've never seen anything like it. We went down to the barracks, met five other girls and headed downtown.

New York had gone madly wild, and I guess we were, too. We walked down Broadway, singing most of the way. It wasn't bad until we got to about 53rd St. when things began to get more packed and rougher. All traffic was stopped below 52nd St. and Broadway, so we took to the streets there. By the time we hit 46th St. we felt pretty mangled. We were still four blocks from Times Square but it was getting to be too much for us, so we cut over to Fifth Avenue and continued on down. Things were crowded there, but a little saner.

By 11:30 P.M., we were worn out. We stopped at St. Patrick's Cathedral, then headed slowly home. Had something to eat along the way. Got in the tub and soaked my poor feet for half an hour before going to bed.

If I hadn't been so tired, I'd liked to have gone down this morning to see the mess that was made of Times Square. We did nothing but read the papers and talk for about an hour this morning at work, and then we were told two of the shifts would have today off, and the other two tomorrow. So, I spent a very relaxed morning reading. This afternoon I'm going to see if the Metropolitan Museum of Art is open, or perhaps the Natural History Museum.

Tonight, Mary and I are going to celebrate her birthday.

If I don't let you know to the contrary, I'll be on the same 4:55P.M. train on Saturday.

It's too soon to know how the Waves will be discharged, or what activities will close down. The youngest class at Columbia graduates on November 4th. I doubt that any more classes will be brought in.

See you Saturday,

Love, Ruth

AFTERWORD

Ohio museum volunteers build a vintage B-17 airplane: how you may get involved:

At the time of this writing in 2014, at Grimes Field in Urbana, Ohio, dedicated volunteers at the Champaign Aviation Museum are restoring a B-17 Flying Fortress bomber, christened the "Champaign Lady."

The story began in July 2005 when the "Liberty Belle," a fully restored B-17, landed at Grimes Field. The airplane attracted hundreds of people to the airport, who donated $18,000 to the Liberty Belle Foundation for the opportunity to walk through or ride in the aircraft. Tom Reilly of Tom Reilly Vintage Aircraft, Inc. was impressed and inspired to develop a B-17 restoration project at Grimes Field, and, with the help of the assistant manager of Grimes Field, Carol Hall, contacted Jerry Shiffer. Shiffer was a local business and community leader and private pilot. The project soon was organized. Tragically, that November, Shiffer died in the crash of his Cessna 425 Conquest I. His widow, Leah, and children David, Andrea and Eric resolved to carry out his wish to create the four-engine memorial to World War II veterans.

The task is an enormous one. The hangar holds shelving bearing large crates and bins loaded with thousands of parts. As of 2014, the airplane is roughly halfway complete, being built from the ground up with parts from at least five different B-17s. The cockpit came from a Nevada bombing range, and a rear section was previously used in the 1964-1968 television series "Twelve O'Clock High." More parts were salvaged from the crash site of B-17 44-85505 near Talkeetna, Alaska (approximately 160 miles north of Anchorage) in July 2011. Some of the parts picked up were the tail, a portion of a wing, the left main gear, and three turbo chargers. The inboard wings came from a B-17 used as a test bed, and the forward fuselage and outboard wings were pulled from a search and rescue B-17. The nose was constructed in the hangar, but the turret has an interesting story. In 2010, it was discovered lying under the back porch of a home on Bellevue Avenue in Springfield, Ohio. It was probably manufactured in the 1940s by Springfield's SPECO (Steel Products Engineering Company).

Randy Kemp, a former B-52 crew chief, is the project manager and is the museum's only employee. After serving in the Air Force, he assembled 100 B-1 bombers for North American Rockwell in Columbus, Ohio.

Volunteers, some regular locals, including George Snook and Art Kemp (profiled in earlier chapters), and others coming from long distances are the mainstay of the project. Their generosity of time and labor under the supervision of Kemp drive the project. They use specifications on original drawings to fabricate the missing parts.

Many of the volunteers, such as Norm Burmaster, are the sons of World War II veterans. His father, Stanley W. Burmaster, served as a tail gunner on the B-17, returning home after 25 missions, including D-Day. On D-Day, due to weather and fog, his father's crew dropped their bomb load at an inland point, Honfleur, France, to assist the infantry troops going ashore. His mother was a war bride. An uncle, Lawrence M. Brustrom, who served on a B-24 with the 466th Bomb Group, was shot down July 18, 1944, became a prisoner of war at Stalag Luft 4 and took part in the Black Death March. In October 2010, two busloads of his father's 91st bomb Group and their families toured the Grimes Field museum. Norm said, "I want to be a part of maintaining this part of history, involve young people and educate them on not taking our individual freedoms in the U.S. for granted. We want to keep the memory of these veterans alive, long after they pass away."

The museum sponsors tours for veterans, school and scout groups. It also sponsors a fund-raising gala every year. In April 2013, Capt. Robert "Hoot" Gibson, a retired naval aviator and NASA astronaut, shared highlights from his career as the featured guest speaker. Donations are integral in keeping the project running.

L-R, Art Kemp, Elizabeth Cassen, and George Snook at Champaign Aviation Museum Urbana, Ohio 2013.

In addition to the B-17 project, the museum hangar also displays a B-25 Mitchell, (fully restored and airworthy), an A-26 Invader, a C-47 Skytrain, a Stinson CAF airplane and a vintage Fairchild. For easy viewing, nothing is roped off in the hangar.

One can walk right up to the B-17 project and speak to Kemp and the volunteers.

B-17 restoration project Head Randy Kemp and WW II Veteran Art Kemp, Urbana, OH 2013.

Urbana is located just north of Springfield, Ohio, on Route 68. Admission is free.

Museum hours:
Tuesday-Friday, 9 am-4 pm
Saturday, 9 am-2 pm
Address: 1652 North Main St.,
Urbana, Ohio 43078
Telephone: (937) 652-4710
Website: www.champaignaviationmuseum.org/

Some of the volunteers on the B-17 restoration project,
Champaign Aviation Museum, Urbana, OH.
George Snook (second from left),
Art Kemp (third from left),
Norm Burmaster (fourth from left),
Project Lead Randy Kemp (third from right).

ABOUT THE AUTHOR

Elizabeth Cassen is a retired commercial pilot, having flown world-wide in a variety of aircraft for a major U.S. airline. She and her pilot-husband make their home in Wyoming.

www.TheLastVoicesBook.com